the

WEALTHY

THERAPIST

The WEALTHY THERAPIST

How to Make More Money
So You Can Help More People

JESSICA HARRIS

ILLUMIFY
MEDIA.COM

The Wealthy Therapist

Copyright © 2025 by Jessica Harris

Published by
Illumify Media Global
www.IllumifyMedia.com
"Let's bring your book to life!"

Library of Congress Control Number: 2025920969

Paperback ISBN: 978-1-964251-88-2

Cover design by Debbie Lewis

Printed in the United States of America

This book is dedicated to my little girl, Adeline, so that she knows that she can do anything she wants in life. Go after your dreams, baby girl. All of your wishes can come true.

CONTENTS

INTRODUCTION

THIS BOOK IS WRITTEN FOR therapists—like you—who would like to learn how to make more money, have more free time, and help more people. Done are the days of self-sacrificing, burning out, and living paycheck to paycheck. Time for therapists to enjoy life again and make a bigger impact in this world.

The "wealthy therapist" is able to enjoy their life, enjoy their work, and change more lives because when you're not stressed about finances, you can stress less and perform better. You can also focus your attention on what's most important to you. It's so much easier to help yourself, your family, and society when you are well rested, have massive savings, and are at peace in your day-to-day life.

If the word *wealthy* feels a little uncomfortable for you, you're not alone. But you're in the right place. In this book, I'll walk you step by step through the strategies, systems, and mindset shifts you need to grow your income, attract private pay clients, and build a business that supports your best life.

Whether you're just getting started or you've been in private practice for years, you'll find practical, actionable tools inside these pages to help you create the results you want. I'm so excited for you to dive in!

Here's why I wrote this book:

1. **To help you succeed.** I'd love to support you in my twelve-week program, the Therapist Private Pay Accelerator, where you'll learn exactly how to implement everything in this book, personalized to you and your unique business, and build your dream practice and life. I have helped hundreds of therapists in my program fill their caseload with private pay clients, and I'm on a mission to help tens of thousands of therapists do this too.

2. **To prove what's possible.** I want to show therapists everywhere that they can do anything they set their minds to. If you believe it, you can achieve it, and I'll share both my story and the exact steps that helped me build a thriving, fulfilling practice and seven figure coaching business.

I'm also passionate about giving away as many free tools and tips as possible, many of which you will find in this book. For more free tips, make sure to follow me on Instagram at @empoweringtherapists. I make marketing simple and easy for you. I'll teach you how to work smarter, not harder.

I am on a mission to help therapists everywhere to make good money so that they can help more people, but more importantly so that they can take better care of themselves and enjoy their lives again.

If, while reading this book, you feel called to get support in growing your private pay or insurance practice, message me on Instagram at @empoweringtherapists, and my team or I will get you set up with a free consultation call. I'd be honored to help you.

Let's get started.

Chapter 1

ALL THE ODDS WERE AGAINST ME

WHEN I GOT MY DEGREE in social work, I never imagined I'd one day crack the code to earning multi six figures a year in my therapy practice, let alone $1 million in revenue in one year from my coaching business. Or that I'd have a pink, sparkly car, live in my dream house, and travel the world with my little girl as a single mom. But I did. I discovered the right steps, implemented the right strategies, and it worked.

And guess what? What worked for me can work for you too.

I grew up with so many negative beliefs about money. I grew up with so many scarcity beliefs that money would always run out and that there would never be enough. But I also simultaneously wanted more in life; I just didn't know how to achieve it. Yet.

In eighth grade, I was sitting in Honors English when a couple guest speakers came into our classroom to talk to us about college. As they explained some of the career opportunities and income possibilities that we might consider, something stirred in me. I decided I wanted to be someone who made a lot of money.

That presentation opened my eyes to what was possible. This was the first of several transformative moments in my life as I declared to the universe that I was going to make a lot of money and nothing was going to get in my way. I could feel it in my bones.

Unfortunately, I had no idea how to make it happen. Yes, the desire had been planted to make something big happen in my life, but I had a long way to go.

In fact, I was going to have to undo a lot of limiting beliefs I'd picked up along the way if I was going to have a snowball's chance in hell of making my dreams come true.

Being Conditioned to Be Broke

Let me tell you about my first money memory.

I was about five years old, emptying coins out of my brother's and my piggy banks, counting them on the floor with my parents since they needed every penny they could get to pay the bills. There were quarters, dimes, nickels, and pennies scattered everywhere. We were stacking coins on top of each other, adding it all up. I vividly remember seeing the little stacks of coins all piled up on top of each other.

I was little and didn't fully know what was going on, but I could feel the tension and stress in the air. I knew my parents feared that there wasn't enough money, and that they needed all they could get. They needed to pay the bills, and I could feel their anxiety.

My parents are wonderful, and I had a great childhood, but lack of money was a constant looming fear for my parents. I could feel the tension in the air many times throughout childhood over there not being enough money. They worked hard, but money was always a concern, and I thought it was just a normal way of living.

To this day, that memory and several others are very vivid and bring up scarcity beliefs I have about money. Those memories taught me core beliefs that money always runs out. That money will always be a constant source of stress. That money is difficult to attain. And that money is difficult to keep. Despite the money I've made, I've still had to work on removing the fear that money will always run out. These beliefs run deep in my body, and I can feel them resurfacing even as I write this.

Growing up religious also led me indirectly to feel a certain way about money. While it may have not been directly stated, there were lots of beliefs around not needing to make more than was sufficient for my needs, that wanting more than I needed was selfish or worldly, that the love of money was the root of all evil, and that money can cause people to do bad things.

I do agree that money *can* cause people to do bad things, but I would say the lack of money causes people to do a hell of a lot more bad things than someone who has an abundance of money. The less money a person has, the more they need to focus on it. The more money someone has, the more they can just enjoy life and serve others more.

While money may not directly correlate to happiness, it sure makes life a lot less stressful.

Flash-forward a few years. I remember sitting in a classroom on my very first day of grad school and being told by my professor that as a therapist I would never make a lot of money but at least I would be able to help a lot of people. Her words didn't surprise me since I'd spent plenty of time researching the average income for therapists and I knew it was not a lot.

I actually remember thinking that I didn't need to make a lot of money since, as a woman, I could also rely on having a husband who worked. I settled for the fact that I would make decent money, live a decent life, and be content with more than I grew up with.

Not long after I graduated, I found myself divorced and raising my eight-month-old baby as a single mom. The divorce was very unexpected—not part of my life plan in the slightest. Just weeks before we divorced, I remember telling my husband at the time how sad it is for people to get divorced when they have children because it means they won't see their babies as much. In fact, wanting to soak up every possible moment with my baby, I stopped working and became a stay-at-home mom.

So to say I was blindsided by our divorce would be an understatement.

I had to find a job in the therapy world and do it quickly. The stress and anxiety of finding employment, putting my daughter in child care, and somehow balancing all life's responsibilities all on my own were daunting.

But I had done hard things at other points in my life, so I knew I could figure it out. I was grateful I had gone to college and grad school, knowing that it gave me better career opportunities than if I had not. I knew I would be okay and be able to take care of my daughter.

Sadly, equally "true" to me were my ingrained beliefs that I would never make a ton of money, that I didn't want to make "too much" money since making a lot of money was "bad," that many rich people were selfish, and that I became a therapist to help people and not to make a lot of money. And I believed all of that until I finally went into my own practice and saw the endless possibilities for making a lot of money while still being able to help a lot of people.

So many therapists are taught to lower their expectations for themselves and put the needs of others first. If you were able to make it out of grad school without negative beliefs around making too much money, then you are lucky. And also rare.

Unfortunately, helping others at the expense of your own needs is a quick road to burnout as a therapist. In fact, I'm guessing you've experienced feelings of burnout at some point in your career journey or are feeling it now. Maybe you've even felt it so strongly you have been ready to throw in the towel and give it all up. But you are here reading this book for a reason, and there is a better way. A way to make more money and work fewer hours. A way to become a *wealthy therapist.*

Many therapists tend to look down on other therapists when they go into private practice rather than stay in agency work. Or when they decide to go off insurance panels. Or when they raise their rates. Or when they grow other income streams.

And the social pressure can get to therapists. It can cause them to fear taking the leap to learn how to make more money as a therapist. Therapists often feel guilty for putting themselves first.

If anything I'm saying resonates with you, you are in the right place. I will walk you through the process of how to make a lot of money as a therapist, why it's okay to make a lot of money, and in fact why you *need* to make a lot of money as a therapist so you can make the biggest impact in this world. Many therapists go into the field to help people, and the truth is, the more money you make, the more resources you have to help others.

It can take a lot of time to unlearn all the fucked-up money beliefs you have developed over the years. I know I sure inherited a lot of untrue beliefs around money and had to unlearn them all in order to be able to make the income I have today.

Here are some of the beliefs I had to evaluate and eliminate:

- I'm not worthy of making a lot of money.
- Money will always run out.
- There is never enough money.
- Making a lot of money is selfish.
- The more money I make, the more it takes away from other people.
- If I'm not working really hard, money will run out.
- I don't even know how to make money.
- If I make more, people will think I'm greedy or arrogant.
- You have to work yourself to exhaustion to make good money.
- If it feels easy, I don't deserve to be paid for it.
- If I charge more, I'll exclude people who can't afford it, and that's wrong.
- Money will change me, and not for the better.

Relate to any of the above limiting beliefs? It's been quite the journey for me to unlearn these beliefs, and I'm excited to share with you how you can unlearn them too.

The Turning Point

I remember the exact moment I realized something had to change.

I'm a single mom, it was late at night, and I was sitting on my couch, looking at my bank account. I wasn't completely broke, but I sure wasn't thriving. I had done everything I was "supposed" to do. Got the degrees, worked the jobs, helped people. And yet I was tired, stretched thin, and living paycheck to paycheck.

I knew that wasn't the life I wanted. I knew I was meant for more. I had this feeling deep inside my body that I was meant for greatness, but I was never really able to envision it for myself because I didn't know how. But I knew I wanted it. And I was ready to make a change in my life.

That's when I knew I had to start unlearning everything I had ever been taught about money and success.

Unlearning and Rewriting the Narrative

How do you unlearn years (or decades) of limiting beliefs? How do you start believing that financial success is possible for you?

For me, it was a process of doing these three things:

1. SURROUNDING MYSELF WITH EVIDENCE THAT IT WAS POSSIBLE

I started following therapists online who had built successful private pay practices and coaching businesses. I listened to podcasts, read books, and soaked up every bit of knowledge I could. I found coaches and peers who had done what I wanted to do, and I studied their mindset. What did they believe that I didn't? What did they do differently?

2. ACTIVELY CHALLENGING MY OWN THOUGHTS

Every time I caught myself thinking, *I can't charge that much* or *I don't deserve this level of success*, I stopped and asked myself, *Says who? Why not me?* I started writing down every limiting belief I had and replacing it with a more realistic and empowering thought. Instead of "I'm not worthy of making a lot of money," I wrote, "I provide incredible value, and I deserve to be well-compensated for my work." This sounds a lot like cognitive behavioral therapy, huh? Make sure practice yourself what you teach your clients to do.

3. TAKING ACTION BEFORE I FELT READY

You will never feel 100 percent ready to level up. Your brain will always try to keep you safe by convincing you to stay where you are. I had to learn to take action *before* I felt completely comfortable. For me that looked like many things. First, it meant quitting my job to go out on my own and be private pay only; then it meant raising my rates, then hiring other therapists, then starting my coaching business, and finally selling my therapy practice to grow my wildly successful coaching business. It was all scary, but so worth it.

Money Is a Tool, Not a Measure of Worth

Therapists are told that making a lot of money and helping people are at odds. They're not. They go together even more than you may think.

The more money I make, the more I can help. The more resourced I am, the more I can pour into my clients, my family, my team, and my community.

When you make more money, you can:

- take fewer clients and give better care.
- avoid burnout and actually enjoy life.
- offer sliding scale or pro bono work from a place of abundance.

- invest in trainings and education to be an even better therapist.

If you're struggling with guilt around making more money, ask yourself, would you rather . . .

1. be a burned-out therapist, resentful and exhausted, struggling to make ends meet, or
2. be a well-paid therapist, thriving in your work, and able to create real, lasting change for your clients?

Obviously, the second one sounds more appealing, and it can be possible for you.

When you stop viewing money as something bad or shameful, you give yourself permission to create a life that supports you *and* the people you serve.

What's Possible for You

It's easy to think, *Okay, well, that sounds great for others, but I don't know if it's possible for me.*

I want this book to inspire *you* and help you see and envision the success you desire for yourself. And by the time you finish this book, I want your vision to be even greater than you thought possible when you first started this book. I want you to live the happy, successful, and thriving life that *you* deserve.

I feel the success that is possible for you, and I want you to feel it for yourself.

I want you to think for a moment about your future self, the version of you who has unlearned all the limiting beliefs about money, success, and worth. The version of you who enjoys their life, thrives in their work, feels calm, peaceful, and abundant.

What does that version of you look like? What does their life feel like? How do they show up for themselves, their family, their clients?

That version of you exists. And they're waiting for you to step into them.

This book is going to walk you through exactly how to do that. It will teach you how to be a wealthy therapist. And not just wealthy in money (although that is important, too) but also wealthy in all areas of life.

Because you don't just *deserve* financial success; you *need* it to make the impact you're meant to make in this world.

And if I could do it as a broke, scared single mom with every reason to just maintain the status quo, you can do it too.

Takeaways

- You don't have to come from wealth to make wealth; it doesn't matter where you've been or what your upbringing or circumstances have been. You can still make good money.
- Money is neither good or bad; it's just a resource and tool to allow you to have more opportunities.
- You have probably developed several untrue and limiting beliefs around making money; you'll need to identify them and work through them in order to live the life you want.
- Countless therapists have learned a way to beat burnout and enjoy their work again, and you can, too, as you follow the steps in this book.
- You are more worthy of success than you realize, and it's time to stop holding yourself back. Time to become a wealthy therapist.

Chapter 2

TAKING THE LEAP TO START MY OWN PRACTICE

Shortly after my divorce, I started interviewing for different therapist jobs. One in particular really stood out to me, and I ended up getting a job offer. I was so excited!

Until I heard how much the starting pay was . . .

Twenty-seven dollars an hour?! I thought to myself. And this wasn't even a forty-hour-a-week job—I would be paid $27 an hour when I happened to be assigned a client. I hadn't studied for years to be paid just $27 an hour—especially being on one income and needing to pay for childcare. I wanted the job, but I did not love the pay and needed to figure something out.

Luckily, I was able to negotiate my way to a slightly higher pay at this job, and I accepted it, but I quickly realized I did not want to be working for someone else forever. It just made sense that I would need to start my own practice eventually so that I could make a good living for myself and my daughter.

This is embarrassing to admit, but there was a part of me that just wanted to marry a guy who had a lot of money so that I didn't have to work or stress about needing to make a lot of money, but I knew this was not something I could guarantee and ultimately needed to rely on myself to pay the bills. One of the things I learned from divorce is that you never know when life can change; I also learned the importance of not solely relying on someone else.

And my post-divorce dating adventures did not give me much confidence in relying on someone. Things would be going well for a little, and I would think, *Great, this is the guy to settle down and marry, and I won't have to stress so much about working*, and then in the blink of an eye, it would stop going so well, and I'd know I needed to move on. Anyway, I digress. I could write a whole book about my single mom dating adventures, but that's for another time.

Working for Someone Else

Working at a private practice was not as bad as I thought it would be. I loved my boss, I loved the clients I worked with, I loved the flexibility, and I loved not being micromanaged.

In the past I had worked at residential treatment and rehab centers and even the Utah State Prison, all of which I loved, but having a baby and working forty-plus hours a week with a stressful job was no longer my vision as a single mom, so I loved the flexibility of private practice.

I worked at a private practice during the duration of getting my hours to receive my "L" for my LCSW. I was there for two and a half years and felt grateful for every moment of it. As I was approaching my hours for my license, it made sense for me to look into starting my own practice so that I could make more money while working fewer hours. I knew it'd be a risk, but it was one I felt willing to take.

I had watched my boss run a successful practice, and I wanted the same for myself. She was on several low-paying insurance panels, however, and I wasn't sure I wanted to follow that path. So I started studying what other therapists were doing, and studying hard. In the evenings, after putting my daughter to bed, I would research strategies for growing a successful therapy practice, the benefits of accepting insurance versus having a cash pay practice, marketing best practices, and much more.

One day I came across a podcast that I absolutely loved. It was hosted by another single-mom therapist around my age who had also gone through a divorce and decided to take the leap to start her own cash pay practice. Her story inspired me regarding what was possible as a therapist. She was such a huge motivator for me, and I attribute her story to expanding my vision and moving me out of the scarcity mindset.

I started to realize that I could make good money and be unapologetic about it, and it lit me up. I was excited and knew that if this other therapist could have a successful private pay practice, so could I.

I made plans to quit my job as soon as I got my LCSW and start my own cash pay practice, avoiding insurance panels altogether. It definitely felt like a leap, but I was excited for it and started putting in even more work to make sure I did everything I could to set myself up for success.

When My Mental Health Crashed

Most people hear my story of how I filled my cash pay practice up in four months and then hired six other therapists over the course of the next year, and think I must have just held it all together and had everything going so well in my life, and come up with excuses of why their situation is different.

Well, life was not going well for me at the time of starting and growing my practice; in fact, a couple of months before I planned on launching my practice, my mental health suddenly tanked to the worst state it'd ever been in my entire life.

I'd always considered myself to be someone with good mental health. Sure, I'd had occasional spouts of minor anxiety throughout my life and a brief period of depression when I was in college. But overall, I felt mentally strong and resilient. Even during my painful and intense divorce, a few rough weeks after we separated, I knew it would be for the best and I felt at peace.

So to have my mental health suddenly crash felt very intense and scary. By *crash* I mean having several panic attacks a week (and I had never experienced even one panic attack before), intrusive thoughts galore that felt absolutely terrifying, a constant and looming deep depression, and feelings of intense anxiety all of the time.

Looking back, I can see there were some life events that led up to my out-of-whack nervous system, messed-up hormones, and really bad gut health, all of which triggered my mental health to plummet, but at the time my crash felt unexpected and confusing.

One day, right after running a half marathon, I experienced a particularly severe episode. I called my parents and told them I was having a mental health crisis and needed to go to the hospital ASAP.

On the drive there I confessed to them, "We'll see if I can actually start my own practice soon. I can barely make it day to day at this point."

Sitting in the doctor's office, I held back tears. "I'm a therapist and help other people with their mental health all day. In fact, I'm actually starting my own practice soon. Yet I can't seem to get a grip on myself."

Turns out, I was having a bad panic attack. A really bad one. I thought I was losing my mind. Everyone at the hospital was very kind and reassuring and told me it happens to a lot of people, but I couldn't help but feel shame and embarrassment.

Over the next few weeks things started to get slightly more manageable—until I took some new medication that made things even worse than before. I didn't know rock bottom could be that bad.

And I was scheduled to launch my practice in one week.

Despite how my mental health was doing, I was luckily very high functioning. I had a small handful of clients follow me from the group practice I had been working for and felt too scared to lose them if I canceled on them my very first week in private practice.

So I decided to move forward with starting my practice and seeing clients, and luckily, I went from seeing twenty-four clients a week at the group practice to just six that first week in my own practice, which was good since I needed the extra time to recover and heal. And I was very grateful that I was working a third of the hours while making almost the same amount of money.

The potential felt endless.

Over the coming weeks and months, my mental health continued to suffer, and I lived in near-constant fear I was going to lose my mind at any point. Thankfully, I didn't. And it eventually got easier. I continued to feel stronger as the anxiety attacks, intrusive thoughts, and depression lessened. About a year later they finally completely went away (when I stopped eating gluten and dairy). And during this time my practice was still able to thrive and grow.

I'm not suggesting that my path is for everyone. For some people it would have made more sense to postpone starting their own practice to take better care of themselves. Could I have postponed my launch a few weeks and still been successful? Absolutely.

Here's why I'm sharing my struggles with you. It's easy to see the success of another person and assume they succeeded because their life is easier than yours. But many people have their biggest successes in life during some of their biggest personal struggles.

Whatever is going on in your life, don't use it as an excuse to stagnate. Do what you need to do to cope and heal, adjust the timing of launching your dreams as needed, but don't put them off forever. There is never a perfect time to launch your practice, go cash pay, raise your rates, hire another therapist, start another income stream, or pursue any goal that you want to achieve.

Go after your heart's desires; it just might be the best decision you'll ever make for yourself.

Is Getting Clients Really Possible?

When I first started my practice, I remember telling friends that I knew nothing about marketing or business but that I would hopefully figure it out.

"I have no idea how to run a business, so we'll see how it goes." And when I told my boss I was quitting to start my own private pay practice, she said "Good luck, I know a lot of people don't have luck with private pay." And my thoughts were, "Oh I can't wait to prove you wrong." And to say I did would be an understatement.

After the first nine painfully slow weeks, things started to explode. In fact, in four months I was booked solid.

How did I go from knowing nothing about marketing to filling up so quickly?

The answer is endless hours of studying the best tips and tricks from the most successful therapists—and then endless hours of implementing those strategies consistently. Another secret of my success? Believing deep in my core that I would have a thriving practice. I just didn't realize how quickly it would be!

And now that I have cracked the code on learning how to get private pay clients, I get to teach thousands of therapists everywhere how to do the same. And nothing makes me happier.

Too many therapists simply launch a website and create a *Psychology Today* profile and hope that clients will come. They don't put much work into developing a niche, creating clear messaging, making sure their website actually looks good, doing SEO so that clients can find them, writing a compelling bio for therapist directories, and so on.

I could go on and on about the things therapists don't even think about when starting their practice. And I'm not saying it's the therapist's fault. The truth is that none of what I just described is taught in grad school. In fact, many of us got the message in grad school that starting our own practice is frowned upon and that helping people for pennies until we burn out is the best we can hope for.

We were never taught how to run a therapy practice.

So that's what I'm here for, and that's what this book is for.

The chapters ahead will walk you through all the specifics on how to run a successful therapy practice, how to get clients, how to have a long-term profitable practice, and how to make more money as a therapist in general.

Grab your notebook, and let's dive in.

Takeaways

- It's okay to ask for what you are worth and to ask for more money at a job or raise your fees with clients. You must put yourself first so you can better help those around you.
- Even if everything seems to be working against you, if you have a desire in your heart to do something big for yourself, follow your heart, and the path will be cleared for you.
- Growing a successful six-figure practice does not come easy. It's going to take a lot of sacrifice, effort, time, and working on yourself. Anything that is valuable in life is going to require some sacrifice.
- You might know nothing about business and marketing right now, and that's okay; neither did I when I first started. We all have to start somewhere. With enough time and practice you can be a master at all of this.

Chapter 3

IS IT REALLY POSSIBLE TO GROW A PRIVATE PAY PRACTICE?

———————•————————

"ARE PRIVATE PAY CLIENTS REALLY out there?"

This is a question I get asked *all* the time.

I also hear comments like these from people who have listened to the naysayers and come to believe that their dream isn't even possible:

- "Well, I saw in this therapist Facebook group that people are no longer willing to pay out of pocket for therapy."
- "All the therapists in the building I work in said that things are slowing down and it's not possible to grow a successful practice anymore."
- "With this economy, people are no longer able to pay out of pocket for therapy, so I have to accept insurance now."
- And several other variations of the above.

I have good news. None of that is accurate. While I do hear statements like this *all* the time, I also have people telling me every day about all the new private pay clients they are getting and the success they are having. Especially the therapists in my twelve-week program; they are crushing it.

Sure, it's true that many people are unwilling or unable to pay out of pocket for therapy, but it is equally true that many people *are* willing to pay for something they value, such as therapy.

Before we delve into all the specifics of how to get private pay clients, I want to spend some time sharing with you the endless possibilities of getting clients and growing other income streams. I want to inspire you to believe that it is possible to reach your dreams—because if you don't embrace this belief, you won't take the action to make it happen, or you will half-ass it while looking for excuses to fail. Ever tried something and it didn't fully work? Probably because you were lacking in belief, even on a subconscious level.

It's okay to have some uncertainty, especially when trying something new. But belief and confidence in your vision will help you get results much faster than if you didn't fully believe in what you've set out to do.

Let's look at the three most common myths that hold people back and lay them to rest.

"It's not possible anymore."

Many people have heard that while it used to be easy to grow a successful therapy practice and get clients, times have changed and now it's not as easy as it used to be. Some therapists say that in the past all they needed was a *Psychology Today* profile and they would fill up with clients—but they argue that doesn't work anymore.

And in a way, that's all true. In the past you could get away with having a subpar website, do minimal SEO work, do less marketing, and still get clients.

Today, the need for your services hasn't changed—in fact, more people are open to the idea of therapy than ever before. What's changed is the strategies you need to embrace to tap into a market desperate for the help you can give. And learning those strategies is well within your power.

Thousands of therapists each day are getting new clients who are eager to work with them, and this can be possible for you too. I have personally helped hundreds of therapists fill their caseload with private pay clients, and I'm going to help you do the same.

"No one wants to pay out of pocket for therapy."

Why in the world would someone choose to pay out of pocket for a therapist, when they could use their insurance instead?

Well, there are many reasons actually.

First, some people simply don't have insurance or have poor mental health benefits that don't cover much of the cost anyway. These people aren't even looking for a therapist who takes insurance; they are simply just looking for the best therapist who can help them.

Second, many people have had bad experiences with a therapist in the past, or at least mediocre experiences where they didn't notice much benefit. This time around, they are being extra picky about who they work with. They are not necessarily looking for a therapist who takes their insurance, but a therapist who is an expert in their issues and someone with whom they feel a good connection. And while I'm sure they would be thrilled if that therapist took their insurance, that's not their first priority.

Third, many people either have out-of-network benefits with their insurance or have an HSA/FSA card that they are willing to use for their therapy appointments. So maybe they don't love the idea of not being able to use their insurance, but they are willing to use one of these options to offset the cost a little bit in order to meet with a good therapist who will actually help them get better.

Fourth, some people who are struggling want to get help as soon as possible. They may have called around multiple places, and nobody got back to them. At this point they are just looking for any therapist who seems like a remotely good fit and can get them in soon, and insurance at this point isn't top of mind. They are just excited that someone finally returned their call and was able to schedule them soon.

My point is this: Never assume that clients aren't willing to pay out of pocket to work with you. Many people are more than willing to pay good money for a therapist they feel will truly help them feel better in the long run. It may just take some time to learn how to market yourself so you have enough people calling you and you can fill up your schedule.

"The economy sucks, so now I have to accept insurance."

Yes, the economy struggles off and on, and depending on when you are reading this, the economy could currently be in a terrible spot, or it could be doing okay, or it could be flourishing. The point is, there will be ebbs and flows, and your business does not need to tank just because the economy is not doing well.

There is a caveat here: If the economy truly is in a horrible spot, you may have to do more marketing, or it may take a little longer to grow your practice than if the economy was doing well. But you can still do it. I have helped countless therapists fill their private pay practice even when the economy was not doing great, so I know it is possible for you too.

This doesn't mean that you are trying to get clients who are in poverty, people who have just lost their jobs and have no savings, or people who can barely buy food. While some people are having a hard time, other people are buying homes, booking vacations, spending money on unnecessary things, and investing in themselves. Remember that even in a tough economy, there are people out there who are not struggling and who have the resources to pay for services that are going to give them the help they need.

Don't fall into the panic of social media or the news when the economy is not doing well. This will only cause you to fall even more into the scarcity mindset. What you see online is often a distorted, extreme slice of reality. Social media and news outlets capitalize on fear; that's just how they work. The more panicked or emotionally activated you feel, the more you click, scroll, and stay glued to their content. If you spend too much time reading about how the economy is struggling, you'll suddenly be convinced that everyone is broke, no one is spending money, and starting or growing a business right now is irresponsible and impossible.

When you consume too much of the news or social media, it can also negatively impact your marketing energy. You'll start second-guessing your rates, pulling back from showing up, and questioning your worth as a therapist. The scarcity mindset will creep in, and it's hard to attract clients when you don't think anyone can pay you.

So be mindful of what you're consuming. Set boundaries around news intake. Unfollow accounts that make you spiral. Unfollow Facebook groups where people are saying it's not possible to get private pay clients anymore. Spend more time listening to people who are building, growing, and thriving. Rather than having black-and-white thinking, remember that two things can be true at once. Many people can be struggling financially, *and* many people can be doing well, or at least well enough to pay for therapy.

I get on social media all the time to build my business, but I am not scrolling my news feed to read the negativity. I have been a part of several therapist Facebook groups, but I made sure that none of the groups showed up in my news feed so I didn't have to see the "nobody is willing to pay out of pocket anymore" posts. I don't talk business with certain people. I keep my circle of influence very tight and only consume things that are uplifting to me and help me tap into more of an abundance mindset.

Give yourself permission to shift into the abundance mindset and focus on the truth that there will always be people who are doing well, value therapy, and are ready to pay for what you have to offer.

So What Is the Biggest Obstacle to Starting a Private Pay Practice?

If there *are* private pay clients out there, and insurance and the economy aren't the obstacles you thought they were, what's keeping therapists from starting their own practice?

It's uncertainty.

In fact, uncertainty is one of the biggest things that keep any of us from taking the next step in our life, whether in business or any other area. People would rather deal with unhappiness than uncertainty.

If you're reading this and have already started your own practice, you may be feeling uncertain about the steps you'll need to take to raise your practice to the next level, steps like raising your fees, getting off insurance panels, growing another stream of income, hiring another therapist or admin, or doing more to put yourself out there and market your practice.

It's important for you to create a full vision of what you want to accomplish in life and where you want your business to be so that you are able to live up to your full potential.

Creating the Vision

You are way more likely to grow a successful therapy practice if you first take some time to fully envision the type of life you want to live and to establish your business goals based on the lifestyle you want to live.

Why is this so important? Remember the famous *Alice in Wonderland* quote:

CAT. Where are you going?

ALICE. Which way should I go?

CAT. That depends on where you are going.

ALICE. I don't know.

CAT. Then it doesn't matter which way you go.

Moral of the story: You need to know where you want your life and business to go, so you know where to go next in your business. The more clear and detailed you are in both, the easier it will be to accomplish the tasks necessary to get you where you want to go. You will know exactly what moves to make next and be able to have a clear plan to accomplish your vision even faster, avoiding a lot of the common mistakes people make on the journey of entrepreneurship.

The Type of Life You Want to Live

Determine the life you want to live, and then create a business plan that will help you get there. It's called lifestyle by design. Instead of creating a business and then just accepting whatever lifestyle that business gives you, choose the lifestyle you want and then intentionally plan out your business so that you will achieve your chosen lifestyle.

For instance, when I was first starting my practice, I knew I wanted to be able to spend as much time with my daughter as possible, and I knew I wanted to make at least $10,000 each month so that I would have enough to cover all my bills, have extra money for fun and savings, and be able to travel. I didn't want to work Mondays or Fridays so I could prioritize those days with my daughter. Since I was divorced and shared custody with her dad, he often had her on weekends, so I wanted to have as much time with her during the weekdays as possible.

I also knew I wanted to continue to grow my income beyond just $10,000 a month since my vision for my life was big. Growing up without a lot of money, I wanted to shift that scenario and be able to have an abundance of money in order to buy a nice house, nice car, and nice travel. I also knew I eventually wanted to increase my income so that I could keep upleveling my lifestyle.

As you determine the type of life you want to live, be clear and specific with your goals. The more detailed you are, the easier and more likely it will be to achieve your goals.

Write down the type of house you want to live in and in what type of neighborhood, the type of car you want to drive, what you want your day-to-day life to look like, what you envision doing on weekends, the types of trips you want to go on, how much money you want to put into savings each month, how often you want to be working, what type of work you want to do, etc.

Your Business Goals, Based on the Lifestyle You Want to Live

Okay, so now that we have your lifestyle goals down, take a moment to figure out the type of business you want to grow in order to meet those goals. Do the math, crunch the numbers, and be specific.

For instance, if you want to hit $8,000 a month and work four days a week, how many clients do you need to be seeing a day and at what price point?

Or what about $10,000 per month or more?

Maybe you want to take four weeks off each year and only see eighteen clients a week. How much revenue would that bring in? Let's look at different rates you could charge if you wanted to be cash pay only.

Let's do the math. I like to see the numbers, so let's crunch them.

$150/session – 18 clients/week – 48 weeks/year = $129,600/year
$175/session – 18 clients/week – 48 weeks/year = $151,200/year
$200/session – 18 clients/week – 48 weeks/year = $172,800/year

And this is taking four full weeks off and only seeing eighteen clients a week!

Laying it out like this and being specific can really help you determine how much money you need to make each week in order to live the life you want. And if you need more money and you don't want to work more clinical hours per week, you could raise your fees, hire another therapist, start therapy intensives, or add another income stream.

How to Create Your Dream Business

Now that you have your lifestyle planned out and your business goals written down, it's time for the fun part: how to implement your plan.

Grab a pen and paper and buckle up, since that is what the rest of this book is about. We will walk through all the specific nitty-gritty steps to help you grow your dream business so that you can live your dream life and become a wealthy therapist. I can't wait to share. Time to change your life.

Takeaways

- In order to get private pay clients, you must believe there are actually clients out there willing to pay for therapy. Your beliefs will determine what you accomplish in life.
- People will always need therapy. Even if it takes more work or takes longer to grow your practice than it may have in the past, people still need therapy.

- It doesn't matter what the state of the economy is; there will always be people who are doing well and people who will make it work to pay for therapy.
- Stay off certain social media pages/groups and the news, or at least limit your content if you are following anything that will encourage a scarcity mindset.
- Don't let uncertainty hold you back from taking the leap to go after your dreams. Take action now.
- Write down all the specifics of what you want your dream life to look like; this will help you to be able to come up with a clearer business plan so you can make it happen.

Chapter 4

HOW TO GET PRIVATE PAY CLIENTS TO WANT TO WORK WITH YOU

WHEN YOU ARE GROWING YOUR practice, getting new clients all boils down to two things:

1. creating a compelling message so that the right people want to work with you
2. helping those people find you

It's really that simple, and everything you do in marketing will fall into those two categories.

In this chapter we'll talk about the first point, crafting a practice and message that compels people to want to work with you.

Getting Clients to See the Value in Working with You

When I first started my private practice, and even months beforehand, I knew I would need to do everything to stand out compared to all the other therapists out there. Especially being private pay only, I knew I needed to do even more than what the average therapist was doing. I wanted to fill up, and I wanted to fill up quickly.

I also had a huge vision to hit at least $10K each month, which is something that I never thought I could hit before having my private practice. But as I was doing the math, I realized that hitting $10K-plus months while only working three days a week was well within my reach.

I was also committed to spending a lot of quality time with my daughter.

Big goals, right?

So how did I begin filling up my calendar? I learned exactly how to get private pay clients to want to work with me and see the value in paying my fee. This chapter will be an essential part in laying the foundation for you to do the same. People need to see the value of working with you so that they are willing to pay the money you charge.

This chapter will cover all the things I did when starting my practice and what I have taught thousands of therapists to do. It will specifically apply to getting private pay clients to want to work with you, but will also apply if they are insurance clients, coaching clients, intensive clients, group therapy clients, retreat guests, etc. I'm going to help you get clients—of all kinds—to see the immense value that you offer so they are willing and eager to work with you to get life-changing results.

Having a Strong Niche

Before you can show a potential client all the value you offer, you need to figure out your niche. After all, riches are in the niches. Meaning that people are way more likely to pay good money for someone who has a niche and shows themselves as an expert, versus someone who says they can help anyone with anything. People are willing to pay more for an expert.

So many therapists are afraid to have a niche, but it's like the saying goes: "If you speak to everyone, you are speaking to no one."

I can't tell you how many therapist websites or therapist directories I see that just have huge lists of all the challenges they help with, such as anxiety, depression, trauma, relationship issues, life transitions, grief, and the list goes on and on. While you may have experience in all these areas and can indeed help with all of them, it doesn't give someone with crippling anxiety, or a failing marriage, or bipolar disorder, etc., the confidence that you are the number one expert to address their area of need if you are talking about how you help with everything.

I know many therapists are so afraid to limit themselves. They are afraid that by niching down they are losing out on clients, but I promise you the opposite is true. By niching down, you will actually gain tons of clients.

When you know your niche, you can speak directly to the kind of client you want to work with. You can name their struggles, speak to what they're feeling, and offer the kind of help that feels relevant to them. That's when someone reading your website or hearing about you thinks, *Yes, that's exactly what I need.*

People are way more likely to pay for therapy (especially private pay) when they believe you really understand them. When they feel understood, they're more willing to invest in getting the help they've been looking for.

It doesn't have to be complicated. Start by asking yourself these questions:

- What kind of client do I love working with?
- What kinds of issues do I feel confident helping with?
- What transformations feel the most rewarding to me?

That's your starting point. Your niche can grow and evolve over time. Don't fall into the panic at the thought of niching down, fearing that you will be stuck forever in that niche and won't be able to help with other issues too. You just need enough clarity to start speaking to the right people in a way that helps them see the value of working with you.

It's also important to have a niche that focuses on what clients are looking for and what brings them to therapy, rather than focusing on modalities or more vague or unique things that people aren't actually searching for. Keep it simple. Keep it focused on some of the most common things that bring people to therapy.

Here's a list of some of the most common reasons people pursue therapy:

- Anxiety and constant worry
- Depression or persistent sadness
- Relationship issues or breakups
- Low self-esteem and self-worth
- Life transitions (career changes, becoming a parent, divorce, etc.)
- Burnout, stress, or overwhelm
- Grief and loss
- Past trauma or abuse

- Difficulty setting boundaries or people-pleasing
- Feeling stuck, lost, or unsure of purpose

Now, it's okay if your specialty doesn't fully fall into one of these categories, but my guess is that if someone is reaching out for therapy, they are likely experiencing at least one of those things, if not several. Keep your niche creation process focused on the reasons people are actually coming to therapy.

How to Create Your Niche Statement

Once you've spent some time reflecting on who you love helping and what struggles you're confident addressing, it's time to come up with a niche statement.

A niche statement is a simple sentence that sums up
- What kind of client you help
- What you help them with
- The outcome or transformation you guide them toward

It doesn't have to be perfect. It doesn't need to include every single thing you do. But if someone were to ask you what types of clients you work with, your niche statement should be able to clearly articulate it. "This is who I work with, and this is how I can help."

Here's a simple formula you can use to write your niche statement:

"I help [specific group of people] who are struggling with [specific problem or challenge] so they can [specific goal, transformation, or result]."

Let me show you a few examples so you can see how this works:

- I help anxious overachievers stop people-pleasing and start trusting themselves so they can feel calm, confident, and in control of their lives.
- I help new moms navigate postpartum depression and the mental load of motherhood so they can feel like themselves again.
- I help high-conflict couples repair trust and rebuild connection without screaming matches or the silent treatment.
- I help LGBTQ+ young adults struggling with anxiety and self-worth feel confident setting boundaries and building a life they love.

See how these are clear and direct? As a potential client, you immediately know if it applies to you or not. And more importantly, if someone is in that group, they're going to feel seen and be way more likely to reach out.

Now it's your turn.

Try plugging your ideas into the formula. You can try out a few versions. Don't worry about making it sound fancy or getting it perfect. Start with what feels true and clear. You can always revise it as you go.

Here are a few prompts to help you brainstorm if you are still stuck:

- What kinds of clients light you up?
- What patterns do you see in the people who get the best results from working with you?

- What are the specific problems or pain points they come in with?
- What types of transformation do they walk away with?

Once you've drafted a niche statement, try saying it out loud. Imagine introducing yourself to someone at a networking event or writing your "About" page on your website. Does it feel authentic and confident? Does it clearly communicate who you help and why?

If yes, you're on the right track.

And remember, you can change it as you get clearer on who you're best at helping and what kind of work lights you up the most. What matters most is this: When someone hears or reads your niche statement, they should be able to say, "Yes, that's exactly the kind of help I've been looking for." This is how you start attracting the right clients who are excited to work with you and willing to pay your full fee.

Once you have a niche, it becomes so much easier to show people why you're the right therapist for them. Your content, your website, your social media, even your consultation calls will flow better because you're not trying to be all things to all people. You're just being you, helping the kind of people you're meant to help.

Now that you have your niche (or at least a rough idea), let's talk more specifically about how to speak to the pain points of your clients and the solutions they so desperately desire.

Speaking the Language of Your Clients

This is where a lot of therapists get tripped up. We're trained to think and talk in therapist jargon—"attachment issues," "emotion regulation," "trauma informed care"—but that's not how your ideal client talks. That's not how they search for help on Google or talk to their friends about what they're struggling with.

Instead, they might be saying things like these:

- "I feel like I'm in such a funk and can't get out."
- "I can't stop overthinking every little thing."
- "I keep feeling like I am self-sabotaging my relationships."
- "Why do I keep putting everyone else first?"
- "I'm successful on the outside but miserable on the inside."

This is the kind of language you want to tap into. When someone reads your website or social media post and sees their exact thoughts written out, they feel an immediate connection. It builds trust and they start thinking, *Wow, maybe this person really gets me.*

I can't tell you how many therapist websites I have read through where they talk so much about themselves and their modalities, rather than showcasing language that relates to their clients.

For instance, instead of saying, "I use an attachment-based, trauma-informed approach to help you heal relational wounds," you could say, "You might find yourself pulling away or clinging tightly in relationships, and not knowing why. We'll figure that out together so you can feel more secure and connected and stop self-sabotaging your relationships."

How to Determine Client Language

How do you figure out what language they are using for their pain? Ask yourself how your client would describe the following:

- What keeps them awake at night?

- What struggles run through their mind all day every day?
- What prompted them to reach out to you?

And if you have any past client intake forms, you've got a lot of the language your clients use right there, in their exact words. Pull up the part of the intake form where it says what they are needing help with, and copy and paste all of them into a document. And then see if you find overlapping themes or patterns. Or simply just pick from the clients you love working with and see what they are saying. If you don't have access to any past client intake forms, think of what they say on a consult call or what they say in the first session when they talk about what brought them to therapy.

Then, equally important, you want to offer a glimpse of the solution they are seeking by using the language they use to describe how they *want* to feel.

Ask yourself, if a client could wave a magic wand and change their life, what would they want that to look like? How would they describe how they want to feel? What's the biggest change they want in their life?

Now you're not just using their own language to talk about their pain; you're using their own language of hope as well. You're helping them envision what they desire in their life. And you're spelling it out in simple and relatable terms where they are thinking, *Yes! That's exactly what I want!*

Here are some phrases that may resonate with a potential client:

- "Imagine finally being able to say no without guilt."
- "What if you could stop spiraling and actually trust yourself?"

- "Time to stop staying stuck in the past and what-ifs and feel excited about your future again."
- "Therapy can help you feel more grounded, more confident, and back to yourself again."

That's what clients are willing to pay good money for—the solutions they will receive by working with you. The hope that life can feel easier, that they can stop feeling weighed down by their problems and become happier.

And when people can have a glimpse of some of that benefit before they've even started working with you, it makes a huge difference. They will be more likely to be ready and willing to pay whatever they need to pay for your services because they already feel known by you.

Every time you're writing content, creating a page on your website, or speaking on a consultation call, use the kind of language that will resonate with your client to describe their pain and the transformation they long for.

When you do this consistently, clients will start reaching out to you consistently, not batting an eye at your price, and become eager and excited to work with you.

Takeaways

- Niche down. The riches are in the niches. If you are speaking to everyone, you are speaking to no one. Determine your ideal client.
- Come up with a nice statement that clearly explains who and how you help, in simple and easy-to-understand language.

- When writing your messaging, turn off the therapist jargon and get into the minds of clients, considering the main struggles they are experiencing and main desires they are wanting, and use their language.
- Figure out the top reasons your ideal clients are coming to therapy and, if your client could wave a magic wand and have things different, what would be different in their life. Then use that in all your messaging.

Chapter 5

THE MOST POWERFUL TOOL FOR CONVERTING CLIENTS: YOUR WEBSITE

Okay so now that you . . .

- have your niche dialed in,
- understand your ideal clients' biggest struggles and desired solutions, and
- have identified the powerful language that will help your ideal client feel immediately understood and known . . .

What do you do with all the info? Where do you put all this great messaging?

The quick answer is "anywhere and everywhere you are marketing."

There are a lot of places where you can publish and promote your messaging so that your ideal client will see it. This will include your Google Business Profile, therapist directories, social media, Google ads, blog posts, courses, etc. We will discuss all of these in depth shortly, but first let's start with the most important one: your website.

Your Website

The main place you will put your messaging will be your website. This is because everything else—your Google Business Profile, therapist directories, social media posts, ads, even your networking efforts—will lead back to your website. Your website is most likely where people will make the decision to contact you.

Your website is the best place to contain all the information on what you do, how you help, and how to book an appointment with you.

Therapists often spend so much time creating a website, but it ends up missing the mark on several components that are essential in order to get clients to want to work with you. And I get it—as therapists we are here to help people, not be a website designer or a copywriter. And having a good website has absolutely nothing to do with the type of therapist you are, but if you have a good website, people will automatically assume, even at a subconscious level, that you are a better therapist and can provide a better level of care. That's how it is for any business: Better websites cause people to assume you have a better product or service compared to those marketed on a bad website. So it's essential to create the best website possible, especially if you want a consistent flow of clients ready and eager to work with you.

Before we dive fully into website optimization, let's make sure your website has all the right pages. You don't need too many pages; in fact, too many pages can make things confusing or overwhelming, for both you and your potential clients.

You really only need four core pages to create a site that converts:

- Home Page
- About Page
- Specialty Pages
- Contact Page

Let's break down each one.

HOME PAGE

- Your home page is the most important page on your entire site. This is where most people will land—and often where they'll decide in the first few seconds whether you're the right therapist for them without even visiting other pages. First impressions are everything.

Here's what should be included:

- A clear headline at the top that says who you help, what you help with, and your location. (This section is commonly known as the hero section.)
- Several sections with short paragraphs and bullet points that speak to their pain and the transformation they want, with several photos and images included to break up the text and make it easier to read.
- Several call-to-action buttons that say exactly what to do next (like "Book a Free Consult").

- Brief intro about you with your headshot, then a link to your About page for more info.
- Links to your specialty pages. (These help people quickly find the service that's most relevant to them.)

ABOUT PAGE

Many therapists make the mistake of turning their "About" page into a mini autobiography. But honestly, people don't care about your credentials right away. They care about whether you understand them and whether you can help.

Here's what your "About" page should include:

- Start with them. Talk about what your ideal client is going through. This builds rapport immediately.
- Introduce yourself in a relatable, down-to-earth way. Why do you do this work? What drives you?
- A little professional background (degrees, licenses, approach), but maybe put it further down on the page.
- Describe your therapy style or vibe. What is it like to sit with you? How can you specifically help them?
- Add a personal touch (a little about hobbies, pets, being a parent, or something that helps them connect with you).
- Give a call to action that links to your "Contact" or scheduling page.

SPECIALTY PAGES

This is where your niche work really shines. Specialty pages (sometimes called service pages) are individual pages that each focus on one issue you help with, like anxiety, trauma, OCD, high-achieving women, couples therapy, etc. Despite having one overall niche, you will break your niche into two to three different pages, to help you speak clearly on each pain point and to help boost SEO as well.

Each specialty page is an opportunity to go deeper with your messaging. You don't want a long list of conditions you treat all lumped together on one page. That makes it feel like you are not an expert at anything. Instead, give each issue its own page, and let that page speak directly to the client struggling with it.

Each specialty page should include the following:

- A headline that speaks to exactly what you do and your location (for SEO purposes), for example, "Anxiety Therapy in Sacramento, CA."
- A few paragraphs describing their pain.
- Real-life language, not clinical terms. (This is where you reflect what they're feeling.)
- What's possible through therapy. Paint the "after" picture. What could life look like with support?
- How you specifically help. (Share a bit about your style or approach and why it works for this issue.)
- Several calls to action, inviting them to take the next step.
- You don't need to write a novel for each specialty page, but it will be easier to rank on Google if you have at least a thousand words per page. Don't feel obligated to do this all at once; start with one page at a time and one section at a time.

CONTACT PAGE

You want to make it as easy as possible for someone to reach out to work with you. The simpler the process is, the more likely you are to book more clients.

Your contact page should include the following:

- A simple, embedded contact form (Name, Email, Number, Message).
- Your phone number and email address so they can contact you right away.
- Your location so they know where you are.
- A call to action or encouraging message. (Example: "I know reaching out can feel scary. I'm proud of you for taking this step. I'll be in touch soon.")

OPTIONAL BUT HELPFUL PAGES

If you want to go beyond the essentials, here are a couple of bonus pages you might consider as your practice grows:

- Blog—great for SEO and building trust
- FAQs—to answer common questions about therapy or your rates

Now that you have an idea of what pages you need, you can start building your website. I always recommend you spend the most time on the home page of your website, since that's where a vast majority of people will go, and if the home page isn't great, they may never end up even looking at any of the other pages. Then you can dive into your "About" page, your specialty pages, your "Contact" page, and then once those are completely done, you can start working on blog posts and other pages if desired.

Website Design

The other very important yet often overlooked part of a website is making sure that the design is on point. Like we talked about, if your website looks good, people will automatically assume you are better at what you do, even though you and I both know your website design experience has nothing to do with the type of therapist you are.

Important aspects to think about in terms of website design are your colors, fonts, and making sure each section isn't too long. You'll want to have short sections to break up the content and you can add several photos and images as well.

You don't need to be a designer. But you do need to care about how your site feels to someone visiting. Is it calming? Is it clean? Is it easy to read and navigate? Does it feel like it was made for the type of client you want to attract?

When I first started my practice and was putting together my website, one of the first things I did was google other therapists in the area to see what website designs I liked and which ones I didn't like. It gave me a very clear vision of what works on a website and what doesn't work. Sometimes when we are just looking at our own site, it's easy to get unclear about what actually looks good or not, but looking at other people's sites always gives us a clearer picture of what looks best. Pay attention to what feels good, what's easy to navigate, and what kind of tone draws you in. Use that as inspiration, not for copying but to get clarity on what works and what feels aligned with you.

A few key other tips to keep in mind for your website:

- Stick to two to three main colors. And make sure the colors look good. I can't tell you how many poopy brown and bad beige colors I have seen on therapist websites, and don't even get me started on ugly oranges.
- Use clear, modern fonts, nothing too swirly or hard to read, and make sure your font sizes aren't too big or too small.

- Keep sections short and digestible. No one wants to read a novel on your home page. Use headers, bullets, and spacing to make it easy to skim.
- Add high-quality stock photos that reflect your ideal client, preferably your ideal client in therapy.
- Use white space intentionally; don't cram too much into one screen. It can feel overwhelming and difficult for clients to read.

Your website doesn't have to be fancy. It just needs to feel professional, clean, and aligned with your message. It should give your potential client a sense of, "Yes, this is the kind of person I want to talk to."

Getting Your Website Found

Therapists often put *so* much time into creating the best website and best messaging, and then get confused why nobody is reaching out. They start to panic by lowering their fees, obsessively editing their website, and then wonder if private pay clients are even out there. But they miss one of the most important steps: getting clients to find them. You could have the best website in the world, but if nobody can find you, then what's the point?

When I first started my practice, I fell into this boat. I spent so much time on my website and my client's pain points that I thought clients would come pouring in. I wondered if my fee was too high or if something was turning people away. But in reality, it was just that nobody was finding me. So I learned how to put in the work of making sure clients could find me—and keep finding me.

Search Engine Optimization

One of the best ways for clients to find you in the long term is something called SEO, or search engine optimization. This essentially means how to optimize your website so you can get to the top of Google, where clients can more easily find you. The next chapter will cover more in-depth ways to get found on Google, but SEO will be an important topic to cover here as well, since as you are building out your website, it will be important to implement the right SEO strategies as you go.

The concept of SEO can feel like a foreign language to therapists at first. I know it did for me. It can feel very overwhelming and very technical, and we aren't going to cover every little detail in this book. But I do want to give you some of the easiest and most beneficial SEO steps, ones that will be easy for you to implement and give you the biggest bang for your buck. These will be the most impactful SEO tips that will truly move the needle without frying your brain or making you want to throw your laptop across the room.

Before delving into the more complex aspects of SEO, I do want to share one of the most important lessons about SEO: Just having a beautifully designed website that speaks to your ideal client and can convert clients will help with SEO. If people are staying on your website for a while and going to multiple pages, it indicates to Google that you have a website that people enjoy and that gives people what they need. And Google's main job is connecting what people want to the best websites out there on that topic.

KEYWORDS

First let's talk about keywords. Keywords are basically the words and phrases your potential clients are typing into Google when they're looking for help.

- "Therapist for anxiety in Denver"
- "Best couples counselor in Utah"
- "Trauma counseling near me"

So your job is to use those words on your website, especially in your headings, so Google can feel confident showing your website to people who are searching what you offer.

This doesn't mean you have to become a robot and stuff the phrase "anxiety therapist in Denver" twenty times on one page. That's called keyword stuffing, which Google frowns upon.

Instead, think about where would be the most natural places to include your keywords. Start with these places:

- Your headings (Especially the big ones at the top of each page! Google pays close attention to these.).
- Your first paragraph.
- Your title tags and meta descriptions (those little blurbs that show up in search results).

Use plain language, be yourself, and work in keywords naturally (don't force them). You're writing for real people first; Google just happens to be eavesdropping.

WORD COUNT

Next up is to remember that your word count on each page matters. I know you might want your website to be short and sweet, but

Google loves content. It needs enough info to understand what your page is about.

If your page is only 100–200 words, Google's like, "Cool, but I'm not exactly sure what this page is about, so I'm not going to show it to anyone." Shoot for a bare minimum of 500–700 words per page, especially on your main specialty pages. If you can go to 1,000 words or more and still keep it engaging, even better.

Don't stress: I know we didn't go to school to become writers. Just write like you're talking to a client sitting across from you. What are they struggling with? What do they want? How can therapy help?

And if writing a full page feels overwhelming, just outline a few sections first:

- What the client is dealing with
- What they want instead
- How therapy helps
- What working with you is like
- A call to action (how to get started)

Boom. You've got yourself a page.

UPDATING YOUR SITE REGULARLY

It also makes a big difference for SEO when you regularly update your site. Google doesn't want to send people to outdated sites. It wants to know that you're still active and in business. So regularly updating your website, even in small ways, tells Google, "Yep, I'm here and ready for clients."

Here are a few easy ways to keep updating your site:

- Update your home page or specialty pages every month with some additional content or updated client struggles you're seeing.

- Add a new blog post at least monthly.
- Update your pictures if you find ones you like better.
- Add new services, if applicable.
- Even just tweaking your "About" page or refreshing your calls to action counts as updating your site.

And this isn't just about SEO. Keeping your website current helps ensure that you have the best and most updated content that is most applicable to the type of client you want to attract. It keeps your website fresh and not outdated.

INTERNAL LINKS

Another simple tip that helps with SEO is adding internal links, aka linking pages within your site. This is so simple but so good for ranking high on Google. On your anxiety therapy page, say something like this:

"If you're also struggling with perfectionism, check out my page on self-esteem therapy here." And link to it.

Or on your home page, have a little spot with your headshot and a little about you, and then say, "Learn more about your therapist," and link that to your "About" page.

It helps Google understand how your site is organized, and it also keeps potential clients clicking around and staying longer on your site (which also helps your Google rankings).

Phew, I know that was a lot of ground to cover, and I know SEO can feel like one more thing on your never-ending to-do list, but remember, this is one of the best long-term strategies you could apply for your business. Once you set up your website well, it will keep working for you behind the scenes while you sleep, parent, rest, or binge-watch Netflix. And this is one of the many reasons I love helping therapists get found on Google. Do all the tough work up front, and then it just keeps growing while you live your life.

You don't have to do everything perfectly. You just need to do enough so that Google is like, "Oh, hey, this person helps anxious women in [your city]. Let's show them to people searching for that."

And just like that, your dream clients start finding you, even while you sleep.

Takeaways

- Creating a good website will be one of the most important things you will do in terms of getting clients to see the value in working with you.
- Your home page is the main page that people will go to on your website, so make sure it's a good one.
- People subconsciously assume that if you have a better website design, you will be a better therapist, so make sure to spend the time on a good website design.
- Learning how to get to the top of Google with SEO is one of the best long-term strategies you can invest in for getting clients consistently.

Chapter 6

HOW TO HELP PRIVATE PAY CLIENTS FIND YOU

I PUT SO MUCH TIME and research into learning how to get private pay clients at my practice, but things weren't happening as quickly as I wanted. I believed it would work, but I also experienced a lot of worry. Nobody was reaching out to me at first. Minus a couple new clients, it was about nine weeks of crickets, and I started to wonder if growing a private pay practice was possible. It's frustrating to put so much work into making the best website possible, so much work into messaging, and then have nobody reach out. But I stayed strong and kept going, remembering that so many people needed therapy; I just needed to get them to find me.

I learned very quickly that business is not easy. If it were easy, everyone would do it. But it's not easy, so not everyone does it. Growing a six-figure practice takes work, and as long as you're willing to put in the work, and the right kind of work, it will happen for you. Everyone has a different timeline, but it will happen.

Things Are Picking Up

"Once the new year comes, then clients will start pouring in."

Or at least that's what I kept telling myself.

I told myself that calls were slow because of the holidays and that once the new year started, my calendar would fill up. But the first week of January came and went and still no calls.

It was about ten days into January, and all of a sudden I got the kind of email for which I had been waiting: "New Contact Form."

Someone had filled out a contact form wanting to work with me, and when I looked at her information, she seemed like my ideal kind of client. Yay!

I conducted the initial consultation call with her that night as I was driving home from the office, and I remember feeling so excited to be able to work with her.

Our schedules didn't initially line up. I was renting office space on Wednesdays and Thursdays, but she was only available to meet on Saturdays. Determined to make this work, I frantically texted the owner of the building I was leasing to see if I could also get the office on Saturday. Eventually we got everything synced, and I started working with this client.

I was very excited to have a client on my schedule weekly, someone who was my ideal fit as a client, and someone who found me on Google. It looked like my marketing was working, and I was stoked.

The following week came and went with no new calls, and the panic kicked in again, but I was just grateful to have a new private pay client who wanted to meet weekly. She was a great fit for my areas of expertise, and I was very excited to help her on her healing journey. I was just wondering when it would happen again.

Then the next week something exciting happened: I got two new full-fee clients in one day! I was thrilled and couldn't believe it was happening! One of them told me they were impressed with all the good reviews that I had on Google, and the other one told me she found me on Google, and I was the only person to finally answer the phone. They were both so grateful for my prompt response and being able to get them in immediately.

It was working! All the hard work I had put in had *finally* started to pay off. People were finding me on Google and reaching out to work with me. It felt like I was actually going to be able to fill up my cash pay practice at some point without needing a backup plan, and I was so grateful.

The next week things were getting even better. Someone found me on *Psychology Today* and said my profile spoke to them; then somebody else found me on Zocdoc, and I had a couple new people find me on Google again. They all wanted to book immediately.

Wow, this is happening fast! I thought to myself.

All of a sudden new clients were coming out of the woodwork! Sure, there were also plenty of people who left messages then never got back to me or weren't a good fit in some way. But I had equally as many people reach out who were a great fit and booked with me.

If you're wanting to build your practice, you're probably wondering how I went from an empty calendar to having a weekly influx of new clients reaching out to me. There are many steps that go into this. This chapter will cover all the best ways to get clients to find you in the first place. This is one of the hardest steps for many therapists, since they put so much time into making a website or creating a therapist Instagram page or creating therapist directory profiles, only to never get people to find them. Let me share my main strategies for getting clients to find you.

Where Are Clients Looking for a Therapist?

Now that you have a better idea of who your ideal client really is and how to talk to their heart, how do you get them to find you?

There are so many different strategies, such as social media, passing out business cards, cold calling doctor offices, networking events, therapist directories, websites, SEO, etc. Every therapist business coach seems to be recommending different approaches and different places to market; it can be really difficult to know where to begin.

I'm all about working smarter and not harder. So you don't need to implement every strategy under the sun just hoping that something sticks. Instead, let's figure out the most effective strategies that give you the biggest bang for your buck. And let's keep it simple.

It's all about going where most clients are in fact looking for a therapist. What is the number one place that people go, a place that doesn't require a huge continuous effort on your part, and a place where you can see results faster than other strategies?

Google.

Google is the main place where I was able to grow such a successful private pay group practice, and where I have helped thousands of therapists to get found as well. It's a place where people are already looking for a therapist. There are thousands of people searching for a new therapist on Google every single day. So let's get you found there.

Google is also nice because once you implement all the best strategies and build a solid foundation, you don't have to do a ton of upkeep—compared to needing to make posts, reels, and stories on social media every day.

And once you build a strong foundation, you can have a steady stream of clients flowing in. It can take time; I'm not here promising instant results, but it comes. When all the right steps are in place and you give it enough time, it always comes.

ChatGPT is also rapidly growing in popularity for where clients are looking for a therapist, and everything you do to get found on Google will also directly help you get found from ChatGPT. So it's a really good bang for your buck. I will talk more specifically on ChatGPT in the next chapter.

Google Searches

It's very easy and convenient for people to pull up Google on their phone or computer and start searching for a therapist in their area, where they are then flooded with so many options and resources.

To discover what potential clients will see when they are searching, I tell therapists to do a little exercise. Simply pull out your phone and type in "therapist near me" and see what comes up.

Typically, what comes up is first a "sponsored" section, which basically is where people are paying for Google Ads. This is a strategy you could implement, but I always recommend organic marketing first so that you are not wasting money until you know whether your website will convert clients. Most of the time people end up not needing Google Ads anyway, unless maybe they are hiring new therapists and want clients faster, but even then it's not an absolute necessity.

The next section on Google that typically comes up is the Google Business Profile section, which is the section with the maps where people can see your business name, reviews, and exactly where you are located on the map. A Google Business Profile is the gold mine for getting clients to find you because it pulls up near the top when people are searching, it's an easy way for clients to see a bunch of therapists clumped together rather than having to sort through several pages of Google, and it typically doesn't take too long to rank high there.

The next section to pull up on a Google search is typically *Psychology Today*. *Psychology Today* is a great way to get clients to find you because it shows up at the top of a Google search, and so many clients love searching through *Psychology Today* because it gives them a lot of options to quickly sort through.

Other therapist directories show up on Google as well, but they typically rank much lower. It's still a good idea to see what other therapist directories are showing on page 1 of Google so you see what your clients are seeing. Some of the other therapist directories that show up are TherapyDen, Zocdoc, Good Therapy, Mental Health Match, etc.

Lastly, several different therapist websites show up. They are sprinkled in with more ads and therapist directories, but the bulk of the options will now be several therapist websites. This is not the only place a website will be important, because Google Business Profiles and therapist directories will also lead to your website. But it's very important to do SEO to get your website to show up on page 1 of Google, since many people skip right past ads, the Google Business Profiles, and therapist directories, and want to go straight to the websites. If you want to have your website pull up at the top, that's where SEO comes in that we talked about in the previous chapter. So if you have not applied those SEO strategies yet, go back and apply them.

Thousands of people are searching every day for terms like "therapist near me," "couples counselor in (city/state)," "therapist for anxiety," etc. So what better way to market than by going exactly where clients are already looking for a therapist.

So how do you get found on Google? First and foremost, do the Google search I mentioned earlier to see what clients will see when they are looking for a therapist. Plug into Google "therapist near me" or "therapist in (city, state)" or "therapist for (insert your specialty)."

This will help you see what is specifically coming up in your area. You will be able to see what ads are ranking the best, what Google profiles are at the top, what therapist directories are pulling up for your area, and what other websites you are competing with. Once you do this, you only need to figure out how to get to the top in your area. Let's break down each point so you know how to get to the top.

Google Business Profile

Getting found on a Google Business Profile is my absolute favorite way to get found on Google. If you are unsure what a Google Business Profile is, it's the spot on Google that shows the map with all the different businesses, and it shows each business's location, reviews, and a link to click on the business's website. Just type "therapist near me" on Google and you will see it. It's my favorite because it shows up at the top, takes very minimal work on your end to rank high, and you will show up more quickly on Google with your Google Business Profile than with trying to rank for just your website.

Ever since COVID, many therapists have decided to make their practice virtual only, which is incredible for convenience for both you and your clients. I will say, in my experience most clients prefer in person (which is why whenever people freak out about AI taking over therapy, I remind them that most people don't even want virtual therapy, let alone AI!), but there are still tons of people who are willing to do virtual therapy, or even prefer it. It just might take a little more time to fill a virtual practice than an in-person one.

Honestly, if you are just starting out or just really struggling to get clients, I would recommend getting a shared office space where you can rent out an office a couple of days a week for pretty cheap. That's what I did at my practice, until I filled up completely and needed to hire other therapists, which is when I switched to a full time office, but more on that later.

GETTING VERIFIED

Even if you decide you will always want to be virtual, you can and should still get a Google Business Profile. Google has made it much more of a hassle to get verified now than it was in the past (*verified* meaning that Google has verified your physical address and will allow you to appear in a Google search) and who knows where it will be by the time you are reading this book.

People used to be able to get a virtual address and have no problems getting it verified, but nowadays Google usually requires that you film a video of your office space to show Google you are using an actual office space.

Also, some therapists who create a Google Business Profile will hide their physical address and just list a service area instead, but this is *not* recommended. You must list an actual physical address if you want a good chance at showing up at the top of Google. If you are just virtual and don't have an in-person office, I recommend one of two things:

1. Using your home address. I know people don't love this idea because they don't want clients knowing where they live. But just remember that most people can Google you and find out where your home address is anyway (I know it's creepy and I don't like it, but it's the reality). And also remember that nobody sees a therapist office on Google and just shows up. It's different from a restaurant or a walk-up business where people show up without calling first. For therapy, people make appointments.

2. The other option is using an address of another therapist in the area, typically for a small fee of about $15 a month. For this option, just reach out to therapists you know and see if they will let you use their office address if you pay them a small fee. This could be a great option because it also builds an even stronger networking relationship to refer clients to if needed, and if you ever truly need to use an in-person office for any reason, such as offering an in person therapy intensive, you already have a great option.

Once you have a plan in place for an address, Google may make you jump through hoops and verify the address with a video, often telling you that in the video you must have permanent signage. For this, just go on Amazon and find a sign where you can get your business name engraved on it, then temporarily hang or duct tape it to the door. Follow the rest of the instructions Google tells you to do, and boom. You have a verified Google Business Profile, aka one of the best things you can do for getting clients to find you.

Okay, so now that you have a verified profile, let's do anything and everything to get you to the top.

HOW TO OPTIMIZE YOUR PROFILE

First thing: fill out every single section of your profile and update it consistently.

Start with the following:

Your business name (Use your name plus "therapy" or "counseling" if that's already not a part of your name), your phone number, your website, and your business hours. For your business hours, don't just put in the hours you are seeing clients; put in the hours you are willing to take phone calls. It's essential to have a wide range of hours, because if you only see clients until three p.m. some days, but a client is Google searching therapists at four p.m. and your profile says "Closed" since it's past the hours you put in, they could move on to someone else. So if you are fine taking calls between nine a.m. and six p.m., then list those hours instead.

Next, write a business description that sounds like you're talking directly to the client you love working with. Mention what you specialize in. Use some keywords that your ideal clients might type in (like "online therapy for women with anxiety" or "grief counselor near me"). This helps Google know who to show your profile to, and it also makes your dream clients go, "Wait, that's exactly what I need."

Next, choose the right categories. Your primary category should be something like "Mental Health Service," "Psychotherapist," or "Counselor"; pick the one that best fits what you do. You can also add more categories like "Marriage Counselor," "Online Therapist," etc. Don't overthink it; you're simply helping Google understand what kinds of clients should see your profile.

Next up in helping you rank higher on the algorithm is adding photos. The more, the better. Add a couple of headshots. If you don't have one yet, take a photo by a window with good light and a clear background or take one outside, and have someone else do it for you so it doesn't look like a selfie. Then add a couple of photos of your space, a cozy chair, a plant, a calming quote. Whatever feels like you. Google loves when you add photos, and potential clients feel more connected when they can see who they might be working with.

Next, and I consider this to be one of the most important things for both the algorithm and your credibility, you need to get reviews, lots of them. No, not client reviews; it is unethical to ask clients for reviews. If they want to leave a review on their own, great! But don't ask for them. However, you are allowed to ask colleagues or people who know you well for reviews.

I would send a simple message to any and every therapist you know, or even just other people who know you well, saying something like, "Hey, I just listed my business on Google and was wondering if you'd be willing to write me a review? No pressure if not, but if you would like to, let me know and I can send you the link!"

There you go, a simple, no-pressure message. You can even exchange reviews with other therapists you know. And FYI, these reviews aren't meant to be written by people pretending to be clients; they are simply reviews of your character in general, and people can address in their reviews that they are a colleague of yours.

I recommend getting to ten reviews as quickly as possible, and then getting up to at least twenty reviews or more if you are in a super populated city and your competitors have tons of reviews as well. You don't need to ask for them all at once, but getting at least ten as quickly as possible will definitely help your ranking, as well as make a huge difference for your credibility.

Then, post an "update" at least once a week. The button that says "Add update" is a spot where you add a post that looks like a social media post. You can add any photo and then a tiny blurb below it with keywords, like "If you are struggling with the loss of a loved one, reach out to a grief therapist in Kansas City, Missouri, today." Simple. These posts don't need to take longer than five minutes. Most people won't even see your posts, but it will do wonders for the algorithm and getting you to the top of Google.

You can use any photos you have, use a template in Canva, repurpose stuff from Instagram, your blog, or just write a few quick tips. Here are some examples:

"3 signs you might be emotionally exhausted"

"What to expect in your first therapy session"

"Why setting boundaries feels so freaking hard (and what to do about it)"

This shows Google that you're active, and it also builds trust with people looking you up.

One last thing for your Google Business Profile: Make sure your name, address, and phone number are the same everywhere online, on your website, *Psychology Today*, TherapyDen, wherever. If your name shows up as "Still Waters Therapy, LCSW" in one place and "Still Waters Therapy" in another, or your address is different by one number, Google gets confused. And when that happens, you get bumped down in rankings.

There you have it. All of the best tips for getting your Google Business Profile to the top of Google.

Therapist Directories

Now let's chat about how to get clients to want to work with you from therapist directories. And before we begin, what are the most important therapist directories to be on? Well, the ones that pull up the highest on Google, because these are the ones clients will see first. The main one that always pulls up on top in Google is *Psychology Today*. Some other common ones are Zocdoc, Good Therapy, Mental Health Match, TherapyDen, Zencare, just to name a few. Since *Psychology Today* is the most popular one, we will specifically focus on that platform here, but all the tips apply to other directories as well.

There are so many therapists on each therapist directory, which is why therapists often get frustrated they are not getting any clients from directories. But as long as you can go above and beyond to get people to stop the scroll and actually look at your profile, you will get clients. There are a few different ways to stop the scroll.

Let's put yourself in the client's shoes again. There are three different things that clients first see as they are scrolling through *Psychology Today*, even before they get the chance to click on your profile: your headshot, your name, and the first four lines of your bio. With this in mind, let's make them compelling.

HIGH QUALITY HEADSHOT

Your headshot is one of the most understated yet most important parts of your profile. If you don't think people are super picky about headshots, go through *Psychology Today* as if you were needing to book an appointment with a therapist, and you'll be surprised at how big of an impact headshots can be. It's not about how you look; it's not a beauty contest. It's instead about having a warm and welcoming presence—and making sure the photo is high quality. You don't want your profile photo to look like a selfie, be blurry, have a chaotic background, look unwelcoming, or feature anything else that would make it look low quality or make you look not friendly. You want people to be able to feel they'll be safe to spill their deepest, darkest parts of themselves to you. And having a high-quality headshot just makes people feel like you are more credible and better at what you do.

Getting professional headshots is always a bonus, but if you are wanting to save money, don't stress about it needing to be professional. Instead, just get someone to take a photo of you on their phone, turn on portrait mode, make sure you have good lighting (which you can often find outside), and then boom. You have a headshot. Take a few, and then ask family and friends which one they think is best. This is going to make such a big difference in the long-term growth of your practice, so make sure it's a good one.

COMPELLING BIO

Next up is making sure the first four lines of your *Psychology Today* profile are very compelling. We want people to be like, "Yes, that's me. Let me click on this profile to learn more." This is where your niche comes in. Once you have in mind your ideal client, you want to think of their absolute biggest struggle—the main reason your ideal client would reach out to you. For the first part of your bio, focus on one type of ideal client, not all of the different types of clients you work with. Just one niche, one main struggle.

Then, come up with a very clear and potentially clever or compelling way of speaking to that struggle. It is typically best when you write a sentence or two speaking to what your ideal client is struggling with and then go into who and how you can help. No need to waste the precious first four lines of your intro talking about who you are, your name, welcoming them, or talking about how you are passionate about helping people. Get straight to the point.

My favorite way of coming up with a compelling hook is by using ChatGPT. I simply type into ChatGPT that I'm a therapist writing a bio for my *Psychology Today* profile. I tell them my specialty and my ideal client's main struggles, and then I tell them to write a really compelling intro or hook for me. If you've never used ChatGPT before, it's magical. It's free, no need for the paid version. You can use it on your computer or get the app on your phone, and you will be amazed at what it can do. You can tell it to make the intros funnier, more professional, more casual, shorter, longer, etc. It will give you any variation you like. Once you find something that fits, add any of your own words and plug it into your profile.

I never recommend just copying and pasting from ChatGPT to your profile, since people can often tell if it's written by AI, and it often sounds overly cheesy and not as authentic (although AI keeps getting better). Instead, use it for ideas and then make the bio your own.

FIFTEEN-SECOND VIDEO

Another way to get more people to see your profile is by adding a short video to your profile. It doesn't have to be fancy, just fifteen seconds of you speaking directly to your ideal client. Let them see your face, hear your voice, and get a feel for your energy. You can say something simple like, "If you're feeling anxious, overwhelmed, or just tired of holding everything together, I help people like you slow down and find real relief. Reach out today to book a free consultation call."

I know therapists cringe at the thought of adding a video, and they put it off for as long as possible. I know it can feel awkward and uncomfortable. It's something that therapists often put off for so long, rather than just getting it over with. Just know that it really helps the algorithm and is well worth it.

The video does not need to be perfect, and it's okay if you need to redo it twenty times. Trust me, I've been there. A video is just a great way to build trust quickly and gives people a reason to choose you over the dozens of other profiles they're scrolling through. It really does make a difference.

ENDORSEMENTS

Another great and often overlooked way to boost your profile is by getting endorsements. You can ask a few colleagues, friends from grad school, or therapists you know to write a short endorsement on your *Psychology Today* profile. You can offer to do the same for them, making it a quick win for both of you. These little blurbs build credibility and also help the algorithm rank your profile higher.

UPDATING YOUR PROFILE

You'll also want to keep your profile active. The *Psychology Today* algorithm tends to favor therapists who are regularly updating their profiles. Every so often, take a minute to update a sentence or two, add more photos, or add new things to your profile. Even small changes show that you're engaged and available and will help you to get found by potential clients.

And there you have it—all of the best ways to get found on Google—and how to get found consistently so that potential clients keep reaching out to you.

Takeaways

- Google is one of the main places that people go when looking for a therapist, so it's essential to implement all the best ways to get to the top of Google.
- Do a Google search as if you were a client, and see what potential clients see on Google when looking for a therapist.
- Get and optimize a Google Business Profile as quickly as possible, and get colleague reviews if you want to start ranking.
- Make sure you are updating your *Psychology Today* profile regularly and getting it optimized.

Chapter 7

MORE WAYS TO HELP CLIENTS FIND YOU

I THINK IT'S CLEAR BY now that getting found on Google is the best way to consistently get private pay clients and fill your caseload, but there are of course other ways to market yourself as well, so let's touch on them.

ChatGPT

As technology continues to evolve rapidly, people are increasingly turning to AI over Google to search and navigate the internet. But don't panic, this doesn't mean all your efforts to be discovered by Google search engines is not as important. Actually, ChatGPT luckily pulls *directly* from Google, so all your hard work on Google will now help you get found on ChatGPT also.

Increasingly, people are using ChatGPT to search for therapists, and this will only grow in popularity as time continues. I have had so many people in my twelve-week program lately tell me that they are getting found on ChatGPT, so it's important to know the strategies to get found.

One of the main sites where ChatGPT gets information about therapists is *Psychology Today*, as well as other popular therapist directories like TherapyDen. These directories can include your location, specialties, treatment approaches, bios, and more. To have correct information about you show up in AI searches, keep your directory profiles updated and active, use keywords clients will be searching for, and make sure you are very clear on your specialties. For example, instead of just talking about how you help people with overthinking, also spell out that you help people with anxiety. You can still go into detail about the overthinking piece, but people are more likely to ask ChatGPT to find them a therapist for anxiety than they are to talk about the specifics of their symptoms.

Another place ChatGPT finds therapists are local therapist websites, which is why doing SEO helps with getting found not only at the top of Google but also on ChatGPT. Make sure you are clear on your city and state as well as your specialties, so that when people are searching what you offer, ChatGPT can easily find you.

ChatGPT also looks up Google Business Profiles and reviews, so consider these things very important. Make sure you can get to the top by being very consistent with optimizing your profile.

Word of Mouth

Another common way that people tend to get clients is through word of mouth. It's a super easy way for people to find a good therapist to work with. If a friend, family member, or another professional is referring someone to you, it makes them way more likely to reach out to you, and it's great for clients when the trust is already there.

Word of mouth can be great, but you may have experienced going to networking events, handing out business cards, or emailing and cold calling a bunch of doctors or other professionals, with no results. You end up getting no clients even though you felt like you had so many good conversations and people said they would refer to you. So what went wrong?

It's common to get word-of-mouth referrals from people you have known for a while, but it's rarer to get referrals from someone you met only once, because typically when you engage in "networking," you talk to people once, maybe send one follow-up, and then never talk to them again, even though you are still expecting referrals.

People are simply way more likely to refer to people they have known for a while, such as therapists from grad school, therapists you have worked with in the past, current or past clients, friends or family you know well, etc. You may have noticed this yourself, that you naturally get referrals from people who know you well, but rarely get referrals from providers you've only connected with once or twice. You will need to nurture the relationship for a while before expecting referrals.

So how do you nurture relationships with new networking connections you have just met? First, make sure you get their contact information so that you can stay in contact with them. And follow them on social media if possible. Then the nurturing process will depend on the type of person or business you are networking with.

For instance, if you met another therapist in private practice, you could get lunch with them sometime, do a virtual meet-up, text them about future networking opportunities, collaborate with them on an event or workshop of some kind, stay in contact through social media, etc.

If you connected with a doctor's office, physical therapist office, yoga studio, etc., you could offer to drop by coffee or lunch to them sometime and then bring in fliers advertising your services. You could also offer to do a free speaking event depending on the organization. And you could occasionally remind them of the services you offer through email or dropping off a holiday treat.

Overall, word of mouth can be a great way to get new clients *if* you are willing to continue to nurture relationships, and then remember that many word-of-mouth referrals will just come in naturally from people you already know, especially if you continue to stay connected with them.

Social Media

Social media is another way to find clients. One thing to keep in mind with social media is that when people are on social media, they are typically on there for fun or for mindless scrolling, not to look for a therapist. And the few times someone does connect with a therapist, the chances of you being licensed in the state they are in is not very high. It will take some work and consistency to get found on social media, but it can happen. Let's talk about the most effective strategies so that you are getting the best bang for your buck.

FACEBOOK GROUPS

One of the most effective strategies for social media is joining local Facebook groups that appeal to your ideal client. This takes away the location issue since you will only be joining Facebook groups for states you are licensed in. For instance, if you work with a lot of moms, there are typically many mom Facebook groups in each state. You could also join small business networking groups, health and wellness groups, relationship groups, etc. Just search Facebook groups in your area and other states you are licensed in; there are endless possibilities. You can also join local therapist groups as well, but just keep in mind that many times they are oversaturated and it takes more work to find your ideal clients within those groups, but it still occasionally works.

After joining some relevant groups within your area, I would then recommend commenting on any posts where people are asking for a therapist or talking about their struggles. I would search the word *therapy* or *therapist* and other related words to see if anyone has ever asked for referrals for a good therapist, and then you could comment, even if the post was made months ago. If the group rules allow, you could even make a post sharing that you are a therapist, explaining who you help, and offering your website. The key here is to come from a genuine place of adding value, rather than a desperate spot where you are spamming people and desperately trying to get clients.

PERSONAL SOCIAL MEDIA

Next, I would also occasionally post on your personal social media that you are currently accepting clients and share your website. Obviously, you can't work with family and friends, but you could share that if they know of anyone who needs therapy, you would love to work with them. This helps you stay top of mind to your personal network, which is where the best word-of-mouth referrals come from anyway.

This is how I got my very first private pay client at my practice. I posted on my personal Instagram and Facebook profiles, and it led to me working with someone weekly at my full rate, ultimately for the entire time I had my practice.

BUSINESS SOCIAL MEDIA

The last thing I'll say about social media is that if you love growing a therapy Instagram page, then go for it. It's not the most recommended technique, although I know it works for some. It just typically takes so much more work with not nearly as many results. One of the reasons it's tricky is that you can only work with people in the state you're licensed in, yet people find social media profiles from all over the world. I'm not against people growing a therapy Instagram page, and I know several people who have gotten clients from their page. A therapy Instagram page can be a great addition, but if you want long-term growth at your practice, make it your priority to get found on Google.

If you do decide to grow a therapy Instagram page, you will just need to be very clear on your niche, even more specific than you would need to be on Google. You will need to follow all the messaging tips that were covered in this book as you create your content, and then you will need to be consistent. You can't just post once a week and expect clients to come pouring in. You should be aiming to post at least three to four times a week, share your call to action, and most importantly be creating the type of content your ideal clients would want to see. It must be super relatable.

Takeaways

- ChatGPT is starting to become a greater vehicle for finding clients, so remember all the work you are doing on Google will make a huge difference, and be sure to make the small adjustments to get found on ChatGPT.
- Networking and word-of-mouth referrals can be another way to get clients; just make sure you are nurturing the new networking connections you make if you expect to get referrals from them.
- Social media can be an added bonus to get clients; just remember most people are on these platforms for fun and not necessarily looking for a therapist. This does not need to be the number one place you spend your energy. But if you have the extra time, go for it.

Chapter 8

STRATEGIES THAT WILL KEEP YOUR PRACTICE GROWING

OKAY, SO WHAT TO DO next in growing your practice? Chances are that as you implement the belief system from chapter 3 and the strategies from chapters 4 through 7—and give it some time!—you will start getting clients.

If you're not receiving new clients yet, not receiving them as quickly as you'd like, or even if you're receiving a good amount of clients but don't know where to go next in your business, this chapter is going to give you tons of additional strategies.

Or perhaps the flow of clients isn't an issue for you, but you need more money or more free time. I have the same good news for you. This chapter and the remaining chapters will paint a clear vision of what to do next to have a practice and business that keeps on growing, while giving you the maximum amount of money and free time you desire.

Finding the Right Balance Between Consistency and Burnout

I notice one of two things when therapists are growing their practice and finally implementing the right strategies:

1. They implement good strategies for a month or two, get busy or distracted and lose focus, then get frustrated when clients aren't coming in.

2. They implement good strategies so consistently that they get to the point of burnout and exhaustion. Driven by fear, they believe they must constantly be working in order to get clients—and that if they take a break, they'll lose everything.

Let's cover how to tackle both of these issues.

NOT BEING CONSISTENT ENOUGH

If you fall into the first category, while sustainability does mean it's good to take breaks and pace yourself, consistency matters too.

When you're a few months into your practice, you typically won't have to do nearly as much as when you started, but even after you get some momentum, there is upkeep and maintenance required if you want to keep getting clients. And when it comes to SEO and continuing to increase your visibility online, Google loves when people are actively making updates. So do other directories like *Psychology Today*. They want to be displaying therapists who are actively looking for clients, not outdated people who haven't touched anything in a few monhs and may never respond to client inquiries.

This doesn't mean you have to do updates forever; you may get to a point where you have done so much that clients keep pouring in and your calendar is so full that you don't necessarily need more clients. But while you are working on getting full, raising your prices, getting off insurance panels, or hiring, let's be consistent.

There are updates you should be doing weekly and updates you should be doing monthly. Let's break it down.

WEEKLY UPDATES:

- Google Business Profile—Get a new colleague review; post one to two updates.
- Website—If your website is not currently looking the way you want it to yet, spend at least one or two hours making necessary changes.
- SEO—Do one thing related to implementing SEO on your website (go back to chapter 5 if you need reminders on what these are).
- Local Facebook Groups—Create a post or comment on posts relevant to your specialty.
- Networking—Reach out to one new provider in your area or follow up with past providers you've contacted.

MONTHLY UPDATES:

- Google Business Profile—Update or add to your description, tweak your hours just a little, add a new photo.

- Website—Add or update a new section on your website, such as the home page, about page, a specialty page, or blog pages.
- *Psychology Today*—Update or add to your bio (can be a small change), get another therapist endorsement, add a new photo (until you have a few photos).

These updates will not only show that you are active; they will also help build your credibility and make sure things feel in alignment to where you want them to be.

DOING TOO MUCH WORK

Now I want to speak to the people who are doing too much to the point of exhaustion and burnout. These are my perfectionists, people who think their income is tied to the amount of work they are doing, people who, quite frankly, are a lot like me. Or at least how I used to be.

It doesn't matter where you are in growing your client base. Whether clients are starting to trickle in or the floodgates are open, give yourself permission to take breaks. You are allowed to take breathers. Go ahead and take evenings and weekends off.

You're in this for the long haul. Make it sustainable. Take care of yourself along the way.

I get it because I have been there. I relate to all of this way too much! And I know from my own struggles and experiences that there is another way. An easier way. A way that involves way more self-care and relaxation and enjoyment of your life.

Use the same checklist I provided above in the previous section. Whether you need more consistency or more rest, it puts you on a good pace and is a reminder you don't need to be always working. Check them off and move on. Turn off your computer, turn off any work notifications on your phone, unplug, and breathe.

Notice how the weekly checklist doesn't say "Spend five hours a week on your website;" it says spend one to two hours max. It doesn't say you need to reach out to ten providers each week; it says one. It doesn't say you must master all of SEO by tomorrow or else; it says do a single thing related to SEO. Once you finish the steps for that day or week, stop. You're good. Clients will come, I promise.

Finding the Right Balance Between Being Patient and Trying New Things

You may or may not be getting as many clients as you'd like at this point. Maybe you've gotten some, maybe you've only gotten one or two, or maybe none at all. It's easy to get frustrated when people are telling you, "You just need to give it more time," and you're like, "I've given it lots of time and nothing is happening yet." I want to share some insights on the balance of truly giving it more time and also making some shifts when things genuinely aren't working.

GIVING IT MORE TIME

Sometimes it really is about more time. When I started my practice, I spent months beforehand building out my website and getting my marketing strategies ready, and I still had nine weeks of crickets once I started. And nine weeks is faster than most. Many people have three to four months of crickets, and even longer if they are not implementing the right strategies. Just know that it is normal to experience a waiting game.

If you just launched your website a couple of months ago but have implemented zero SEO strategies, you need to implement SEO strategies and then give it about three months at least before you start expecting clients. If you don't have a Google Business Profile or haven't gotten any reviews or done anything to optimize it, get it done ASAP, and then expect that it will likely be at least two months before you can start expecting results from it.

The day you plant the seed is not the day you eat the fruit. Remember that. Keep watering the plant daily, and it will grow. Even when you can't see it yet, you are building strong roots.

TWEAKING YOUR MARKETING EFFORTS

If you feel like you've been patient but know something isn't working, consider tweaking your marketing. Perhaps your headshot doesn't make you appear approachable or your website is somewhat poorly designed; you may not be doing SEO as well as you think, you may not be using messaging that speaks as clearly to your clients, or your area could be oversaturated with therapists, so you need to get way more colleague reviews than you would if you were in another area.

I know it is frustrating if you are feeling like you are doing *mostly* the right things with no results, but remember that even one thing being off could throw the whole thing off.

If an airplane is even one degree off, just one, you will greatly miss your destination. Pilots talk about how for every one degree a plane gets off course, it will miss its targeted landing spot by ninety-two feet for every mile flown. That's a lot of feet, especially if you are going a lot of miles.

It doesn't mean things have to be perfect—there is no such thing as perfection in building a therapy practice—but you need to be enough on target if you expect to be getting clients, especially if you are wanting private pay clients.

So how do you even begin to tweak your marketing?

A good place to start is by asking family and friends what they honestly think of your headshot and website and messaging. Then ask colleagues. Tell people to be blunt with you. Then go compare your website and therapist directories to those of other therapists in the area. Be on a mission to find the best *Psychology Today* bios and best therapy websites out there. How do your headshot quality and messaging and website design measure up compared to theirs? You can try to self-diagnose any issues as much as possible.

The second thing you can do, especially if you want clients sooner than later and want to start hitting months of $10K or more, or whatever your desired revenue goals are, is to hire a therapist business coach. Hire someone who has been there, done that, made mistakes, can prevent you from making the same mistakes, and can get you clients ASAP. They can catch things that are making a huge difference toward increasing your client base. And they can point you specifically in the right direction for where to turn next.

Finding the Balance Between Hiring a Coach and DIY

My biggest regret in growing my practice is not hiring a therapist business coach sooner. I wasted tens of thousands of dollars on silly things that did not matter or did not help, and I could have gotten even more clients sooner, and I could have been a lot smarter with profit margins.

You can wait six months to start getting occasional clients and a couple of years to fully fill up, or you can hire a therapist business coach and be getting consistent clients in three to four months and be fully booked six months later. Do the math. If you'll make $10,000 a month by having a full caseload—and working with a business coach gets you there six months sooner—*not* hiring a coach could cost you up to $60,000 or more you would've otherwise made. So many people are afraid of the cost of investing, but what about the cost of not investing in yourself. Read that again.

I recommend you hire someone who is or has been a therapist, has grown the type of practice you want, has an expertise in marketing and SEO, is genuinely concerned with your success, has already helped a significant number of therapists, and has incredible testimonials from people who have worked with them.

If you are wanting to grow a successful therapy practice, then I would recommend . . . me. I meet all the qualifications above and would *love* to help you. If you would like to schedule a no-pressure, no-cost consultation call with a member of my team, send me a DM on Instagram at @empoweringtherapists or email me at support@empoweringtherapists.com, and my team or I will make sure it's a good fit and book your free consult call.

My clients get incredible results, and their success only continues to skyrocket long after their time in the program.

I can't tell you how many clients I've worked with who say that they feel like they've already done everything and are afraid my program would teach them nothing new, but decide to join anyways and realize they were missing the mark on so many things and are so glad they made the investment.

Let's get experts to have their eyes on your strategies so you can diagnose why you are not getting clients and how to get more clients, consistently.

You could also continue working on your practice by yourself without hiring help, but make sure that you are being really consistent and precise with the strategies outlined in this book. Also, be honest with yourself if it's been weeks or months of trying with little to no results; the reality is something is off. The problem isn't the economy or that nobody out there is willing to pay out of pocket—the problem is your strategy. And it's okay to reach out to a business coach for help.

My rule of thumb is that if you are not getting at least two to four new clients a month in your practice consistently, and you still need at least six to eight new clients to fill up, hire a business coach ASAP so your practice can be full and thriving.

Finding the Right Balance Between Taking Care of Your Clients and Taking Care of Your Own Needs

As you continue to grow your business, you will also need to keep redefining your goals and how to achieve them. What got you to where you are won't always be what takes you to the next level.

The goals will obviously be entirely different depending on what stage you are in building your business. Some therapists simply want to fill their own caseload and aren't interested in creating a group practice or pursuing other income streams. Some therapists want to hire one therapist, whereas others want to have a huge group practice. Some want to offer intensives in addition to seeing clients, and some want to add coaching. The possibilities are endless. But it's important to redefine your goals continuously as your grow your business.

Even if you simply want to fill your own caseload and nothing else, there are still goals you can redefine. Maybe the amount of money you are charging isn't cutting it anymore, and you need to raise your fees just a little. Maybe you want to work fewer hours, or more hours. Maybe you want to add in a couple of intensives so your clients can see results more quickly and so you can make more money.

I would take some time to visualize your dream schedule, dream income, dream clients; then ask yourself if you are on the path toward those dreams or being led away from them.

This is also your time to give yourself permission to want more. To demand more. We as therapists are often taught to sacrifice and give so much of ourselves to our clients and everyone else and not take the best care of ourselves. It's not just about getting by; it's also about enjoying our life and work. It's time that we as therapists take a stand for what we want, and do it unapologetically. No more need to sacrifice our own needs for someone else.

RAISING YOUR FEES

I am such a huge proponent of therapists raising their fees as needed. Raising your fees can feel like such a big scary thing, when in reality it usually makes no difference to the clients to pay an extra ten to twenty dollars a session, yet it adds up a lot for you! If you are charging $150 an hour and raise it to $160, and you see fifteen clients a week, that is an extra $150 a week, $600 a month, and $7,800 a year! And double that if you raise it by $20 an hour, and so on. So it is well worth it for you to raise your fees. And you are one step closer to becoming a wealthy therapist.

Obviously, do this within reason. I usually like to work with a client for nine months to a year before raising fees, although sometimes it may happen sooner. But you can raise your fee at any time for new clients coming in. For instance, if you are charging $175 and want to raise it to $200 for any new clients coming in, just change it on your website today, and next time you get a call, just remember to tell them your new fee—and do it with confidence. You got this.

ADJUSTING YOUR SCHEDULE

Typically, when someone first starts growing their practice and getting clients, they are just so happy to get any clients on their schedule that they put people in time slots that aren't ideal for themselves.

If you remember a few chapters back, I talked about how I fit someone into a Saturday when I first started my practice. And since then I had started seeing another client on a Saturday as well. So every Saturday or every other Saturday I had to drive to my office. When I first started, this was well worth it to me. Clients were coming in slowly at first, and I didn't want to lose any clients; I also had a lot more free time. Both of those clients were people who weren't free to meet until six p.m. or later during the week, and it was a hard no for me to work past six p.m., because I needed to be with my daughter in the evenings, but a couple of hours on a Saturday was okay to me at the time, and I was so grateful to have those clients.

But as my practice grew and once I had a group practice and a coaching business (we will talk more on that later), I no longer had the capacity to meet with clients on Saturday. It's not ideal to have to move things around on clients, but after about a year of seeing them on Saturdays, I was able to move one to a five p.m. spot on a weekday, and another one we simply just could not work out another day of the week to meet, but he was able to switch to one of the therapists in my group practice, and he loved working with her.

The point of the story is that you get to create your dream schedule. Maybe initially you are seeing clients five days a week, but eventually you want to switch to working only three days a week to give yourself a four-day weekend. Or maybe you were working evenings and you no longer want to see clients past five p.m. Or you want to start your days later or give yourself a long afternoon break.

Many therapists find themselves self-sacrificing and in turn burning out and becoming exhausted. If you want to be a wealthy therapist, you need to make sure you remain in a good state of mind and don't become burned out or resentful. You want to be enjoying your work as much as possible; that way, you will have a clearer mindset in order to come up with the best business ideas to move your business forward. And the whole point of growing your business is to have more time and money to enjoy your life even more.

Takeaways

- Balance is a necessary part of growing your business in the long term.

- It's important to continue to be consistent with your marketing strategies. The day you plant the seed is not the day you eat the fruit. Keep "watering" your business.
- The amount of hours you put into your business doesn't necessarily equate to the results you will get, so don't burn yourself out by working too hard. Just implement the right strategies, and then give yourself a break.
- You may be missing the mark with what you're doing in your marketing efforts. If clients are not coming in after months of consistent work, take an honest look at your efforts and make some changes, or better yet, hire a therapist business coach.
- As you grow your business, it's important to take time to pause and reexamine your business and your business goals. Take an inventory of where you are now and where you want to be.
- It's okay to raise your fees or adjust your hours in your practice. You are allowed to make more and work less.

Chapter 9

TRANSITIONING INTO A SUCCESSFUL GROUP PRACTICE

LET'S GO BACK TO TALKING about how my therapy practice was going. Last we left off, it was finally picking up.

With the slow rate I saw at the beginning, I was fearful it would take a year or longer to fill up my practice with clients. Suddenly the next thing I knew, in four months from starting my practice, my caseload became full. I filled up my schedule with eighteen full-fee, private pay clients each week, and I was thrilled.

Once my practice filled up, the phone calls kept ringing. The contact forms kept getting emailed in. It was incredible.

At that point I had three choices:

1. I could see more clients each week.
2. I could turn new clients away.
3. I could hire another therapist.

As a single mom, I knew I didn't want to spend less time at home by taking on more clients, so option one was out.

And as an ambitious person who had spent so much time marketing and creating a solid foundation for my practice, I also knew I didn't want to turn away clients, so option two was out.

So I decided to go with option number three and hire another therapist.

Before I go on, I do want to make it clear you can still have a lot of success and growth even if you decide hiring is not for you. It does take a lot of work and is not for everyone. If you are getting a steady stream of clients and do not want to hire another therapist to join your practice, your next step could be to start raising your fees for new clients and possibly offering therapy intensives or creating other income streams. Of course, you don't need to do any of this right away. You can also take a break from marketing and just enjoy the new clients at your practice, but as you are ready to continue stepping into the role of the wealthy therapist, there are more options.

When I decided to hire at my practice, I had no idea where to begin. I started googling all the things I needed to do when hiring another therapist. I reached out to my accountant and my lawyer to see what I needed to do and what pieces needed to be in place. I wanted to make sure I was doing all the right things to set myself up for long-term success. In some ways the task seemed very overwhelming, and in other ways it seemed straightforward enough to start. I was also getting several new calls and had no more time slots for new clients, so I was ready to hire.

Looking back, it's crazy how fast things moved. Instead of waiting things out for a couple of months to make sure clients were consistently coming, I just hired. I just went for it and hoped for the best. I just *knew* things would work out. I knew clients would keep coming. I was in the energy of things working out no matter what, and they sure did.

When to Hire

Every practice is different, so how will you know when it's time to hire? Many therapists ask themselves questions such as

"Is it really the right time to hire?"

"Could I keep another therapist full?"

"What if clients just suddenly stop reaching out?"

"Will other therapists really want to work for me?"

"Is it going to be too much work to hire?"

"Why would they pick my small practice over a big practice?"

These are all very common questions, but let's break it down so it doesn't seem so overwhelming or impossible.

You may be able to hire sooner than you think. If your caseload is full, you are turning clients away, or you are consistently getting inquiries for specialties you don't offer, that's when it might be time to bring someone in.

Just know that hiring doesn't have to feel overwhelming. You don't need to fill up the caseload of a therapist you hire right away. You can just be transparent in the interviewing process that you don't know how quickly their practice will fill up (no one does). A lot of therapists are open to starting part-time while they're still working another job or just easing their way back into work. You don't need to have a full caseload ready for them from day one; that's not expected or realistic—just be honest about it.

You may be thinking, *Why would a therapist want to work for me over someone else? What's in it for them?*

Well, if you are a cash pay only practice, or at the very least have a lot of cash pay clients, they will likely be making more per hour working for you than for someone else. A huge perk of being private pay only is how much more you get to pay your therapists. I was so grateful to be able to offer the therapists who worked for me so much more than anywhere else in the area.

Other benefits of working for you could be that you may be able to offer more flexibility and less micromanaging than a big practice. Some people like the feel of a small practice, and you may be able to offer them more of the types of clients they want to work with, less burnout, a better work environment, and the ability to learn how to eventually start their own practice.

So don't sell yourself short.

Once you are ready to hire, you may worry about all the work that goes into it, and I can relate. It is a daunting task at first. I had a million questions.

1. What kind of pay and benefits do I offer, W2 or 1099?
2. How do I find a good therapist to hire?
3. How do I go about interviewing a therapist?
4. What does the onboarding process look like?
5. How do I change or expand my marketing to make this work?

It can be overwhelming to figure all this out at first, so let's break it down.

Pay and Benefits

Before determining how much you will pay your therapists, you will want to break down how much it will cost having a new therapist. Costs to consider include having them on your EHR, workers' compensation, malpractice insurance, company taxes if they will be W2, etc. Consider how much you are paying in rent if you offer in-person therapy, and if you need to rent out another office space.

You'll also need to think about how much time and energy will go into marketing for a new hire and getting them added to your website. Will you pay for their *Psychology Today* and other therapist directories? Consider the time you'll spend on payroll and paperwork and whether you will be supervising them or not. There is also the time it will take to train them and manage questions they will have while they work for you.

All of the above usually ends up taking more time and money than you may think, so take your time to analyze these things before offering a pay split.

A common rule of thumb for pay is to do a fifty-fifty split, but you could do a little less if you will need to supervise them and/or they are a W2 (because of company taxes), and you could do a little more if they are fully licensed and/or a 1099. Just remember, you can always increase your pay as you go, but you can't necessarily decrease it (I mean you could, but your therapists probably won't be happy).

Let's look at an example. If you are charging $150 a session and are cash pay only, don't jump the gun and start paying the therapists too much, say $90 or $100, thinking, *Sweet, I get to make $50 or $60 and won't even be seeing the client.* Take a step back and think about the expenses and time that goes into everything. You can start off by paying them $75 a session, which will likely be way more than they would make anywhere else. Then, after the first few months, if things are going well and profit margins are high, you can always slowly increase their portion.

BENEFITS

You will also want to determine the types of benefits you will offer the therapists working for you, if any. Usually, when you first start out, you won't really need to offer any benefits, as the main benefit will be that they will be paid a lot per session. But some benefits to consider either now or in the future are continuing education reimbursement, health insurance, PTO, 401K, etc. Start slow, and remember that many small therapy practices never offer benefits beyond CEU reimbursement, so do what feels best for you.

W2 OR 1099

You'll then need to decide whether you're looking to hire therapists as an employee or an independent contractor. Independent contractors typically have more freedom in how they work and are responsible for their own taxes, while employees have more structure, benefits, and tax withholding. If you want to set their schedule, require certain hours, or provide materials or training, they're likely considered an employee in the eyes of the IRS. But if you offer more flexibility and freedom, having independent contractors is often the way to go.

This may depend on your state or licensure (so be sure to check with a lawyer or accountant), but typically if a therapist doesn't have full licensure and is still being supervised, you will need to have them be a W2. They are usually not able to practice as an independent contractor, and their hours won't count toward their license. It's nice to have an independent contractor because you don't have to pay all the company taxes, so it will save you big-time on taxes, but sometimes you may have to do a W2 depending on the situation.

How Do I Find a Good Therapist to Hire?

Next step—how did I go about hiring in my practice? Anytime I looked for jobs in the past, I typically went to Indeed. It was always the first job posting site that was always at the top of Google, so it seemed to have the most jobs and the most people searching. So posting on Indeed was going to be my plan. But I decided that before diving into posting on Indeed, it made even more sense to first try my personal network to see if anyone knew of a therapist looking for a job.

I made a story on my personal Instagram profile saying I was hiring another therapist if anyone knew of someone looking for a job; on my Instagram story I mentioned the pay range I would pay them and the flexible hours I would offer. I was eager to see what the results would be, hoping at least one person would reach out, but instead, I got flooded with responses.

I was honored that I had so many therapists to choose from and excited to decide which individual would feel like the best fit.

One therapist in particular really stuck out to me because I'd worked with her in grad school and I knew she was incredible. She was always someone I looked up to. She would be all telehealth since she lived an hour away, which saved office space on my end. She also was just getting back into work and was fine with a very slow buildup of clients. I went through the hiring process with her, and she became one of the first members of my growing group practice. I was thrilled.

In the meantime I was already chatting with another friend whom I also wanted to work with. I had recently reconnected with her and was very excited to work with her since we were friends and she was a great therapist. I knew that she would add a lot of value to the practice. And she was excited to work with me since I could pay her more than she was making at her current job. So I hired her as well.

When you are first looking to hire, I usually recommend seeing if there are any therapists you know within your local network who are looking for work. You can post on your personal social media profiles, either in your stories or as a post. Just share that you are hiring, the approximate pay, the hours or flexibility, and any other important info. Some people are surprised that there are already people in their local network looking for a therapist job, which means they don't have to post on a job posting site.

The next way I would recommend finding a therapist to hire is by posting in any local Facebook therapist groups, sharing your job opening as well as the benefits of working with you in your practice.

If none of that leads to anything, then your next best bet is to post on Indeed and other job posting sites. Just google "therapist jobs near me" or "therapy jobs in (state you're in)" or whatever would be applicable, and see what job posting sites pull up. This is what potential employees will see. Usually Indeed comes up first, but if any other ones seem good near the top, you could post on those sites too.

In all of your posts sharing that you are looking to hire someone, it's important to learn how you can stand out above the rest and really speak to what a potential employee would want to hear. Especially if you are a private pay practice, since you can typically pay your therapists better, you should include a pay range. Include the hours and/or the fact that you're flexible with their schedule. Include any other benefits you will offer, even including simple phrases like "Choose your own schedule," "We have a great team culture," "We don't micromanage," or any other benefits that you think would appeal to prospective employees. This will help your posting stand out above others, making viewers more likely to want to work with you over other practice owners.

Very similar to getting private pay clients, it's important to always show others the value in working with you. Some therapists take months to find a good therapist to hire, but it's often because people can't see the benefits of working for them over someone else.

Interviewing Process

Interviewing therapists and making sure they are a good fit is a crucial part of hiring. It will save you a lot of time and headache if you are picky and only make sure to hire someone who is a great match for you and your practice.

When people make their first hire, they are often nervous and have no idea what types of questions to ask. But rest assured, they don't have to be perfect, and if anything, it's more about feeling out the person's vibe and making sure the logistics match, rather than asking things like "What is your biggest weakness?" and "Name a time when you were at a job and you had to solve a difficult problem and how you handled it." I always hated questions like those.

You are mostly wanting to get a sense of whether the person you are looking to hire is someone you can easily get along with and would be easy to work with. You can also simply ask yourself, would you want them as your therapist? If not, then others probably wouldn't either.

Next, you need to make sure the logistics line up. See if they are okay with the pay, the hours, the start date; figure out if their specialties fit with what you are looking for, etc.

Below are some interview questions to keep in mind. Pick the ones that feel the best fit for you.

- What past therapy job experience do you have?
- Who is your ideal client?
- What types of issues do you prefer *not* to work with?
- What modalities do you use most often, and why?
- What attracted you to our practice?
- What are your expectations around caseload and session frequency?
- What kind of supervision or consultation do you find most helpful?
- Are you comfortable managing your own schedule and documentation in a private pay setting?

Trust your gut through the process, and then once you find a therapist who feels like a good fit for your practice, you can go ahead and offer them the job. Just make sure you are not rushing into hiring because you really need someone and then settling for someone who is not the best fit. If you hire a good therapist, you will have good client retention. If you hire a mediocre therapist, you may not have the best retention. A mistake in hiring could potentially cost you thousands of dollars.

It's typically not about finding someone who has been a therapist the longest and seems to have the best qualifications.

It's more about finding someone who has the best energy, whom you enjoy being around, and who is open to learning and growing.

Onboarding Process

It's so exciting to finally feel like you found a therapist who is a good fit for your practice. Your vision of continuing to step into the role of "wealthy therapist" is continuing to grow.

One of the first steps to getting a new therapist onboarded in your practice is sending them an offer letter to offer them the position. Next, determine how you will pay them, send them tax forms, add them to your malpractice insurance, etc. An accountant can help you with all this to make sure you are doing everything properly. These details will vary from state to state, and this book is not a substitute for legal advice. I am not a lawyer and don't know what is required for your state; I am merely offering general guidelines.

You will also want to update your intake your paperwork and your practice polices and perhaps make an employee handbook.

Finally, set your new hire up for success with a clear process of how you run your practice. Introduce them to your systems (like EHR, scheduling, billing), your values, and your expectations around documentation, communication, and client care.

I know it can feel like a lot at first, but the first hire is usually the hardest, and it gets easier from there once you have your systems in place.

If you would like specific details, templates for offer letters, tax forms, lawyer-approved paperwork, etc., all of that can be found in my twelve-week Therapist Private Pay Accelerator program. Book your free consultation call with a member of my team by sending us a message on my Instagram @empoweringtherapists or sending an email to support@empoweringtherapists.com.

How Do I Change or Expand My Marketing to Make This Work?

One thing I underestimated when I hired two therapists is the stress that comes with making sure their caseloads are full versus your own. Sure, as a private practice owner you want to make sure you are filling your own caseload so you can make a living, but when you hire others, wow, there is a whole new level of pressure to make sure theirs are filling up too.

In hindsight, I wouldn't have hired two therapists at once since the pressure to fill up two felt overwhelming. It all ended up working out, and their caseloads filled up pretty quickly, so it was not a big deal, but this path is not one I'd necessarily recommend to others. One at a time is a lot less pressure.

So how do you begin the process of marketing for the therapists you've hired? It's very similar to the steps you took for yourself, but you want to take it to the next level after you hire other therapists for your practice.

HEADSHOTS

You want to make sure you get a good headshot from the therapists you hire, just like you needed for yourself. I have seen some therapists I've coached who get headshots back from their employees that are nowhere near up to standard. They don't want to make the therapists feel bad, but this is crucial for them if they want to fill their employees' caseloads. You will want to make sure to give your therapists basic guidelines to make sure their headshots are high quality:

- Have someone else take the photo for you, not a selfie.
- Have a background that is simple and not too distracting or cluttered.
- Make sure it is a high-quality photo, aka not blurry.
- Have a warm and inviting smile, try to look welcoming.

If they don't give you a headshot that is up to standard, you can take the headshot yourself or have a professional come in to take the photo. Don't ever underestimate the importance of a good headshot.

There was a time in my practice where we took professional photos for everyone at my practice, so we all got updated headshots. This was great, except when one particular therapist changed their headshot on our website to a much less flattering one. They went from a consistent amount of people wanting to work with them to suddenly hardly any requests over the next few months. When we did get someone on their caseload, the client often backed out last minute. And the only thing that changed during this time period was the headshot photo. Once the headshot went back to the original (which looked much better, in my opinion), the inquiries and retention went back to normal. It was crazy the difference that headshot made.

THERAPIST BIO

The next thing you will need from a new hire is a bio for you to put on your website. When receiving a bio from a therapist, you will want to train them on what to include. For instance, even though it's an "About " page, you want it to be more about how they can help the client, versus all about the therapist. Clients care way more about getting help from the pain they are in than about learning the credentials and experience of their therapist.

This is not to say your new hires can't add details about their credentials and experience; it just shouldn't be the main focus or what they lead with in their bio. Instead, have them lead with the pain points that clients may be experiencing, then talk about how they can help in easy-to-understand language.

Then, as they start to shift in their bio to talking a little more about themselves, make sure the content is still relatable so they capture the attention of potential clients. They can then share more about their experience, training, education, modalities, etc. Bonus if they can also add a little more about themselves personally, such as their hobbies or what they like to do when they are not working.

PSYCHOLOGY TODAY

Next thing you will want to do is get a *Psychology Today* profile up for them, if they don't have one already. You can use the same steps to make sure they have a good headshot and a good bio focused on the client. It will be especially important to make sure the first two sentences of their bio are compelling so people will want to reach out and work with them. Have them add a couple more photos to help with the algorithm as well as any office pics if they will be working in person. They will also need to add a video to their *Psychology Today* profile. Lastly, you will want to make sure they are actively updating their profile at least once a month to help boost themselves on the algorithm.

Of course, they don't need to do all of this perfectly, but if you want them to start getting clients ASAP, you should help them be on top of all these steps, explaining to them the importance of making sure all the pieces are in place. You don't want their poor headshot or bio to impact your income.

It's such an exciting journey to hire another therapist and make money beyond just sitting in your own therapy chair. There are many ways to become a wealthy therapist, and this is just one of them. The next chapters will cover even more ways to make money beyond just sitting in your therapy chair, ways to make a bigger impact and help more people.

Takeaways

- There will never be a perfect time to hire, but if you have enough clients on your caseload and enough money coming in, it might be time to start looking for another therapist.
- Make sure to figure out the expenses of having another therapist on your team before you decide the pay split.
- Check out your personal network first when hiring, and then post on job sites. Share your value, just like you do with therapy clients. Potential hires want to see the value of working with you over someone else.
- The interviewing process is all about making sure you find someone who feels like a good fit for your practice. Trust your gut and don't rush things; having good client retention will be essential for growing a successful practice in the long run.
- If the therapist you hired sends over a headshot or bio that doesn't meet your standards, it's okay to let them know and have them make the necessary changes so that you raise the chances that people will request them.

Chapter 10

THE JOURNEY OF BUILDING A SUCCESSFUL COACHING BUSINESS

RUNNING MY GROUP PRACTICE WAS going well, and we were getting more clients than I ever thought possible. We had a week during the Fourth of July where we got twelve new full-fee private pay clients, all in one week! It was insane. Therapists often fear the summer slowdown, yet we were thriving. On top of that, it was a shorter week because of a holiday, yet clients were still pouring in.

Then in November, right before Thanksgiving, we had our biggest week ever, fourteen new full-fee private pay clients! It was so exciting. I ended up hiring six therapists all in less than a year. I was so grateful.

Making Money Outside My Therapy Practice

In the thick of growing my group practice, I had a thought one day that caught me off guard. On a Friday afternoon, I went to see an outdoor play with one of the therapists at my practice, and as we were talking business, she mentioned eventually wanting to start her own practice. I knew when I hired her that it was an eventual goal of hers to start her own practice, and I always kept an abundance mindset that if any of my therapists left, it wouldn't be a big deal; I would easily be able to find someone else and replace any of the lost income.

For some reason, however, as she was talking about eventually going out on her own, I realized I never wanted to have my income depend on someone else. I wanted to be in full control of my income, to see it go up every month and never take a huge dip because of someone else leaving.

Even before this conversation, I was already thinking about other income streams I wanted to start, and the main one I was thinking about was business coaching for other therapists wanting to grow a successful cash pay practice. When I first started my practice, I was telling everyone, "I know nothing about business and nothing about marketing. Hopefully this works!" Then, all of a sudden, I found a huge passion for business and marketing. I became obsessed with all things business. And I was passionate about teaching therapists that it was okay to make good money.

In fact, a few months prior to that Friday afternoon, I had helped a friend who was starting her own private pay practice. I talked with her about raising her fees and told her all the best marketing strategies that had filled me up with clients in the beginning. When she later applied them herself, her caseload filled up with fourteen to eighteen weekly private pay clients in just two months from starting her practice—it was insane! And it was so fun to help her. It was in those meetings and phone calls with her that I realized I had a huge passion for business coaching, specifically in how to grow a cash pay practice.

Around this same time, a girl I knew with a life coaching business had posted on social media one day that she had just hit $1 million in revenue that year in her business, and I was blown away! She was my age and had seemed to unlock the secrets to making a shit ton of money with coaching, and she wasn't even a therapist. I was so impressed by her that I went to her website to see what she was offering that was allowing her to be so successful; I even ended up on a Zoom call with her to hear what she was doing. She was able to make a million in a year through having a high-ticket coaching program and having incredible testimonials and content that were changing people's lives.

Seeing her massive success lit such a fire under me. I figured if she could do it, so could I. I just needed to figure out what I was going to offer.

Beginning my Coaching Business

About two days after that Friday afternoon conversation with the therapist in my practice, I posted in a popular therapist Facebook group about how I was going to offer discounted business coaching; I explained how quickly my practice had filled up, and I got so many people reaching out to work with me! I was thrilled. I ended up getting about six new business coaching clients over the course of the next week.

As soon as I landed my first coaching client, I was like, *Okay, I guess I need to make this an official business.* I immediately registered my business, chose the business name Empowering Therapists, got my EIN, created contracts, and was ready to go.

As this was taking off, I quickly realized I only had so many hours in the day to see business coaching clients, so I decided I needed to create a course. I wanted to shift gears from the one-to-one model to the one-to-many model, since I could help way more people with the latter, while making so much more money myself.

At this point, burnout was also hitting me hard. I was exhausted in my therapy group practice because I didn't know how to chill out; I just kept hiring and getting more clients instead. I had hired an admin a few months prior, which helped, but I was still choosing to take many of the consultation calls myself because I had a better conversion rate and didn't want to miss out on any clients. I had a hard time letting go of control. Between launching this new business, which added way more hours to my schedule than usual, being a single mom, dating, and taking care of my physical health, my mental health, my friendships, hobbies, it soon became overwhelming.

The first week I started taking on business coaching clients was the first time in my life I ever started having jaw pain; it was pretty intense. I also started having a twitching pain in my neck. All of this was caused by the intense stress and burnout I was experiencing. In fact, as I'm currently writing this book, I am still recovering from the intense neck pain. Even though my stress levels are significantly lower, my body is still catching up.

As I was dealing with all this stress, I knew I needed to chill and stop taking on so many one-to-one coaching clients; I needed to find some time to relax more, but it was hard for me since things kept growing.

I was now on a path to build my recorded course and figure out how much to sell it for. I knew it was going to be such a game changer for therapists, teaching them anything and everything they needed to grow and maintain a successful therapy practice.

As I was on the path to building my recorded course and figuring out all the paperwork I needed to put into place, as well as all the other logistics that go into building a coaching business, I ended up hiring a coach myself, and she ended up changing the trajectory of my coaching career and life forever. She taught me how to change my mindset from the one-to-one model to the one-to-many model with a full-blown coaching program that would change the lives of the therapists who went through it.

Rather than just offering a small recorded course that would be somewhat helpful, I would instead be able to offer the most comprehensive recorded course, several group coaching calls, 1:1 coaching calls, a private group for community support, as well as tons of other support. My coach taught me how to turn my coaching into a twelve-week program so that therapists would actually take action on it, rather than just a cheap course that people never watched or took seriously. I was able to create a program that not only changed therapists' lives but was able to change my life too.

I share all of this so you know what is possible for you as well. I want to teach therapists everywhere that you can do whatever you set your mind to. If you want to be a coach, you can be a coach. If you want to shift gears to another income stream, you can do it. The sky is the limit, and you don't need to fit inside a box telling you what to do.

Taking Off with Coaching

I was so excited to start coaching therapists how to have a successful therapy practice. It was very rewarding and fun. And it was nice to have figured out a way to make money aside from sitting in my therapy chair. It was definitely a lot of work at first, and I was working way more than I ever had in my life, but it was all paying off.

I was curious to see how it would grow, but all of a sudden it took off. People were joining left and right. Less than five months in, twenty people had joined my program. And it has only skyrocketed from there. Even more exciting than that was seeing the success people were having in finding cash pay clients. For many it took some time to see the payoff; it wasn't instant results for everyone. But for anyone who was consistent and implemented the right strategies, whether it was month two or month six, they would get results. It was very exciting to see so many people fill up their caseload with private pay clients; it proved what I had been saying—that it was possible for them as it had been for me.

How to Dive Into Coaching

Many therapists have thought about adding coaching because it allows more freedom and flexibility as well as more income. Instead of doing fifty-minute one-to-one sessions with people only in states where you are licensed, you can work with people anywhere in the world and help them in a variety of ways, such as programs and courses, etc.

If you are considering adding coaching, here are some things to consider:

1. **Ask yourself who you're already helping.**

   Look at the clients, colleagues, or friends who naturally come to you for support. Are there patterns in the kinds of questions they ask you? Do people turn to you for help with building their practice, navigating big transitions, or regaining confidence in their voice? You might already be coaching in some way without realizing it.

2. **Test your ideas with free or low-pressure offers.**

   You don't need a website or perfectly branded Instagram account to start coaching. Try offering a few discounted sessions to people in your network who are curious about coaching. Let them know you're testing things out. See what lights you up, what drains you, and what people want more of. These low-risk experiments can teach you a lot.

3. **Pay attention to what feels fun.**

   Coaching doesn't have to be hard; it can be energizing and fun. If the idea of creating a PDF guide, launching a mini-course, or doing a live Q-and-A on Zoom gets you excited, follow that. The world of coaching is flexible. You get to decide what your coaching looks like. It's a lot different from therapy where you have so many rules to follow. You have so much freedom to explore with coaching.

4. **Start with one person.**

   You don't need to build a program or brand before helping someone. Start with one person you feel called to support in a new way. You'll learn a lot from that experience, and it can help you decide if you are ready to pursue coaching more seriously.

5. **Remind yourself: You're already qualified.**

   Therapists make the best coaches. Yes, therapists often mock life coaches because they try to replace what therapists do. But if you are a therapist yourself, you will be the best coach since you already have the skills. You don't need any certifications. You've sat with hundreds of people through some of the hardest moments of their lives. You've helped people change patterns, build awareness, and grow. Those skills translate beautifully to coaching.

Setting Up Your Coaching Business

If you're ready to dive into coaching, you need to figure out who you will help (your niche), how you will help (services you offer), go make it an official business, and start putting yourself out there (marketing).

Follow the same steps in the earlier chapters of this book to determine your coaching niche and speak on client pain points (you may have the same coaching niche as your therapy niche, which is common).

In terms of coming up with your coaching offer, I recommend having a high-ticket coaching program because that's how you will make the most money and help the most people with coaching. However, this does take a little bit of time to set up, so feel free to start with one-to-one coaching sessions to get your toes wet, maybe start creating a recorded course of all the lessons you would share in coaching calls, and then start putting together some resources that will be valuable to your audience, such as different PDFs and training guides.

You will then need to create a business for your coaching services. Register your business with your state, create an EIN, get a separate business bank account, create an agreement, and you are ready to go.

Lastly, the fun part: marketing and putting yourself out there. I say that marketing is the fun part sarcastically since I know most people do not like marketing and putting themselves out there. But it really does not need to be as bad as you think! When you are passionate about something and have seen it help people, it would be a disservice not to share it with the world.

All the marketing strategies talked about earlier in this book can be applied to your coaching business as well, particularly in speaking to your clients' pain points, creating powerful messaging, having a website that converts, etc.

The main difference, however, will be where you are getting found by your coaching clients. There is still a place to get found on Google for coaching clients, *but* you are way more likely to be found on social media when it comes to coaching. Don't cringe too much yet—I know many therapists don't love the idea of needing to grow their platform on social media, but this doesn't mean you need to do anything that feels inauthentic to you. Be yourself, you have valuable knowledge to share with the world.

I recommend creating a business Instagram account and start with simply finding other profiles of people who are doing what you want to do, then start doing what they are doing in your own authentic way. Not copying what they are doing—that would be unethical but also won't help you since you need your own authentic voice—but simply getting some ideas from others, following along in their strategies, and being consistent. It will be important to show up every single day even when you aren't seeing the results yet. You will then be constantly tweaking what you are doing so that you are implementing the right strategies that get you results.

And there you go—that is a very high-level overview of how to begin and start your coaching business to be able to impact even more lives.

Takeaways

- Coaching can be a great addition to the therapy services you are offering. It offers a lot more flexibility, and therapists make the best coaches.
- If you really want to free up your time and make more money as a therapist, it's important to switch from the one-to-one model to the one-to-many model. Find a way to help people beyond just individual sessions.
- When you are ready to start coaching, you need to come up with your niche, your offer, and strategies to share it with the rest of the world.

Chapter 11

HOW TO TAKE YOUR REVENUE TO THE NEXT LEVEL

AT THE SAME TIME I was growing my coaching business, my private practice was continuing to grow. As exciting as it was to see growth in both businesses, I was feeling burned out and exhausted trying to run two successful businesses and be a good mom.

A Huge Pivot in My Career

At the rate my coaching business was going, I knew I'd eventually sell my practice. I just didn't know when. It was weird even to consider selling my practice since that had never been my plan. I thought I would just manage both and eventually have someone run most of the private practice, but I soon realized that even though I'd stopped seeing therapy clients, there was a huge mental load that went into running and managing the practice, especially since it was doing so well and I wanted that to continue.

I deeply loved my practice; it was my first business. But as it began to feel like "too much," I would occasionally daydream of what it would feel like not to have to manage my practice anymore. It wasn't time to sell yet, however; I wanted to wait until things felt more stable and consistent, since coaching would be my entire source of income.

Then, all of a sudden, things changed.

"Holy shit! I just hit my first $50K month!"

I was in shock. Never did I think I would grow this much so soon. I was only seven months into my coaching business and five months into launching my coaching program. Things were exploding, and I couldn't have been more grateful.

But I was working so much during this time. I was drowning. Every time I remember how busy I was during this time, it makes me want to cry. I can feel the extreme overwhelm I was experiencing all the time. I felt the weight of the world on my shoulders. I was turning down time with friends, had stopped going to the gym, and wasn't traveling anymore. Any moment when I wasn't with my daughter, I worked. Most weeknights I worked past midnight, and I worked every weekend too.

I started to think about my options and what I wanted to do. Sure, I loved therapy, but I was surprised to find that I actually loved coaching way more. And it was way more profitable. Most importantly, it gave me the life of freedom and flexibility I desired.

Selling My Therapy Practice

I suddenly knew what I needed to do. I had such a big vision for my coaching business and changing the lives of tens of thousands of therapists by helping them grow their businesses, so I knew it was time to let go of the thing holding me back from fully achieving this dream.

The thought of selling my practice felt so foreign to me. I remember listening to therapy entrepreneur podcasts who would occasionally talk about selling a therapy practice, and I always felt confused. I would think to myself, *Why would someone ever need to sell their practice after putting so much work into it? Why not just hire someone to run all the logistics?* I couldn't fathom a therapist going to grad school and spending so much time and money to become a therapist, then choose to stop practicing as a therapist. Then suddenly that was me. It made sense.

I'd never sold a business before and had no idea where to begin, but I did a lot of research. I talked with my accountant, consulted with a lawyer, and researched what all the best practices were for selling a business. I also needed to figure out the most important thing: Whom would I sell to?

I thought about what made my therapy practice so successful, and there were two things. One, the marketing was running so well. We were consistently getting so many new clients each week; they just kept coming in no matter what time of year it was. I had done so much marketing work, and it was paying off like crazy. And two, the therapists at my practice were truly great. They were high quality, and clients loved working with them. Clients kept coming back and referring their friends and family, so the growth kept happening.

The therapists were the secret sauce that made the group practice so successful. Sure, I brought most of the clients in the door, but they stayed because they loved the therapists. I would have nothing to sell if it was just me at the practice since I didn't want to see clients anymore, but because there were five other therapists at the time, there was a lot of revenue coming in each month.

I didn't want to just sell my practice to the highest bidder and have them potentially change everything at the practice. I wanted to sell to someone who would keep things relatively the same and then continue to make things better. I wanted to sell to someone where the therapists at the practice would want to stay and continue to enjoy working there.

After much thought, I decided to sell my practice to one of the first therapists I had hired. She was well liked by the other therapists, and I knew she would keep the good culture going. When I told her that I wanted to sell my practice to her, she was thrilled. Over the next few weeks we talked about the logistics, got legal documents in place, determined the value of the practice, and how she would pay me, and within a couple of months the practice was hers.

I was so excited to give the practice to someone who would have more time to build it successfully—and to be able to finally put all my love and attention into my coaching business.

Thinking Outside the Box

Whether or not you end up selling a therapy practice in your lifetime, I share this to let you know that you can think outside the box, that serving clients one on one doesn't have to be the thing you do forever. And even if it is something you do plan on doing forever, you can also be creative with other income streams as well.

It's easy to get caught up thinking there is only one way to make money as a therapist: sitting in your therapy chair and seeing clients one on one. But I want to share with you even more ways to make money. You don't have to feel limited.

I saved this chapter for the end because it's easier to build other streams of income once you are already feeling stable financially, whether you are running your own practice successfully or working for someone else. When you already feel secure in your therapy business, you can give more focus to other streams of income, rather than trying to grow multiple businesses at once.

Most therapists start their private practice to have more time and money, only to find themselves getting caught up in back-to-back sessions with little time to breathe in between, endlessly writing progress notes, and feeling drained from holding space for others all day.

While being a therapist can be such a beautiful thing, it's easy for therapists to feel burned out or think they aren't making enough money. Maybe you are not there yet, and hopefully you will never get there. But if you want to switch things up or find ways to make more money, that is okay too.

I know many of us as therapists don't necessarily feel creative or know how to make money except through therapy sessions, but think of all the skills you have because of being a therapist. You know how to break down big ideas, create transformation, and connect with people in a way that actually makes an impact. Those are incredibly valuable skills outside the therapy room too. Whether it's launching a course, running a membership, coaching other therapists, or even writing a book, you have options. You can shift from getting paid per session to building something that you get paid for on repeat without needing to be in your therapy chair.

For example, if you specialize in anxiety, you could create a self-paced course with the exact strategies you already teach in sessions. If you love helping other therapists, coaching or group programs could be a game changer. Some therapists dive into speaking, launching a podcast, or digital products like workbooks and guided meditations. If you are growing on Instagram, you could start looking into getting brand deals so you can be paid for advertising other products and services. The possibilities are endless once you stop thinking like just a therapist and start thinking like a business owner as well.

You don't have to figure it out all at once; you can start small. Maybe it's a simple PDF guide that answers the biggest questions your clients ask. Maybe it's a live workshop where you teach one of your favorite tools. You don't have to build a huge business overnight; but let's get you started in taking the first step.

Growing Other Revenue Streams

Let me give you a very comprehensive list of some of the most common streams of income that therapists add, to get your brain going with even more ideas:

- Private coaching (e.g., life, mindset, ADHD, parenting)
- Business coaching or consulting for therapists
- Group coaching programs
- Paid speaking engagements
- Online courses or digital programs
- Workbooks

- Membership communities
- YouTube channel
- Podcasts
- Blogging with affiliate links or ads
- Brand collaborations or sponsorships
- Client intake and onboarding templates
- Website templates
- Writing a book
- Clinical supervision
- Yoga, breathwork, or mindfulness classes
- Spiritual or holistic healing offers
- Group therapy
- Retreats
- Continuing education trainings

The possibilities are endless. Take a look at this list and see if something sparks excitement for you. Or select your top five favorite ideas and do more research on them. How much time would it take to grow that income stream? What kind of money is possible? What would the marketing look like? And so on. With more information in hand, it will be easier to boil it down to one or two ideas that you are most eager to start with.

There's not space in this book to dive into distinct marketing strategies for each of the revenue streams I mention above. But I can tell you that all of the marketing strategies I've described in this book can be applied to growing other revenue streams as well; you just need to figure out where people are looking when it comes to those specific revenue streams. For instance, Google and now ChatGPT are some of the main ways people are looking for a therapist, but for some of the other revenue ideas you will need to get found on Instagram, create an email list, or advertise in Facebook groups, on podcasts, etc.

From there, you can apply the strategies in this book to encourage people want to work with you and buy your product or service. You'll need to create your offer, have a niche so you are speaking clearly to a specific population, speak to the biggest client pain points and desired solutions, and then get it out into the world. Be consistent and market your offering daily, just the same way you would need to market your therapy practice. Then continue to fine-tune things as you go.

Adding extra income streams doesn't have to mean quitting therapy (unless you want to). But it does mean having more options, more flexibility, and more financial security. Imagine working fewer hours while making more money, while knowing your work is reaching more people than you ever could in one-to-one sessions.

Most therapists aren't set up on the path for financial success. Insurance companies and agency jobs have set us up for the exact opposite, which is to settle for small amounts of money and to burn out. We're often overworked and underpaid, even though we're in one of the most important professions out there. But when you create multiple income streams, you get to decide what you want to charge. You get to take your business as far as you want it to go. You're not limited to trading time for money in the same way you are as a therapist. You're no longer waiting for a system that undervalues therapy to give you a raise.

Plus, doing something outside therapy often makes people a better therapist. When you're not constantly running on empty from your therapy sessions, you have more energy and creativity to bring to your work. You get to serve your clients and build your dream business. Most therapists describe adding another income stream as something that is energizing and fun—a nice changeup from seeing back-to-back clients.

Remember, though, not to feel the need to do everything at once. Starting and growing your therapy practice is usually one of the best starting places to becoming a "wealthy therapist." Then, as that takes off and feels consistent, you can keep growing from there.

Takeaways

- You have so many options as a therapist to make more money and impact more people. It's time to think outside the box.
- Determine the types of people you want to help, how you best want to help them, and apply the marketing strategies in this book to get yourself in front of your ideal audience so you can get them to want to work with you.
- Remember, don't take on too many ideas at once. Start with growing one thing at a time, whether that be your therapy practice, coaching, or another stream of income. Focusing on one thing at a time usually yields the best results.

Chapter 12

WHY YOUR SUCCESS AND YOUR REVENUE MATTERS

In the introduction, I talked about writing this book because I so badly want every therapist out there to know they deserve a better life and that it's okay to ask for more.

I hope by this point you have a better understanding of ways to grow your practice and income and you believe you have endless possibilities to grow. I hope you are feeling more confident that you can actually do it: that by following the steps in this book, you can grow your income and become a wealthy therapist.

I hope you have embraced a new vision for making more money and why it is so important. Money is not just about the money. Money gives you so much freedom, so many options, and so much more peace in your life.

I used to have such a stressful relationship with money. I always stressed about it running out and felt bad for wanting more. Now my relationship with money is grounded in trust. Sure I still have my moments of panic too. But overall I know it's always flowing to me. I know it can make my life better, and in doing so, it helps me make life better for everyone around me.

Give Yourself Permission to Be Successful Beyond Your Wildest Dreams

So often we are taught that making "too much" money is selfish and takes away from others. But says who? Who are we taking money from? We are not forcing or pressuring clients to work with us. We are providing a valuable service and deserve to be compensated well for it.

Each time you make money, it's because you are providing value to someone, and they are choosing to pay you for that value. And if they weren't paying you, they'd be paying someone else. So why not you? You deserve to get paid for your value and live your life beyond your wildest dreams. You get to do things for yourself you never thought possible before.

Yes, not everyone can afford your fees for your services, and that's okay. You don't need to be for everyone. There are so many therapists out there who take insurance, offer sliding scale or pro bono work, and are simply cheaper than you. Let the clients who can't afford to work with you go to someone else. And if you have a full caseload of high-paying clients, you are in a better position to be able to offer some pro bono services if you desire, as long as you do so without resentment.

Money is neither good nor bad. It is simply a tool that gives you more choices in life to truly live the life you want. Here are some of the benefits to making more money:

- The more you have, the less you have to think about it, allowing yourself to think about things that matter more in life.
- You get to take better care of yourself, which allows you to show up as a better person in the world.
- You get to support family and friends who may be struggling and in need of your help.
- The more you make, the more you can pay those around you. Whether it's your team, someone who comes to clean your house, your nanny, your restaurant server, and anyone else you interact with.
- You get to enjoy life more. While money doesn't necessarily buy happiness, going on fun trips, living in a nice home, getting countless massages, and buying nice things sure makes me happy.

How My Financial Success Has Changed My Life

There are many things I love about money, but one of my favorite things about making a lot of money is being able to travel the world with my daughter. Growing up we couldn't really afford to travel much besides a few road trips. As I got older, I became a poor college student, then a broke single mom, then a broke therapist. That all changed when I started my therapy practice.

I could finally afford to travel and take my daughter on her first trip. We went to Disneyland for both of our first times, and we became hooked. It's been such a special experience to be able to take her to Disneyland, and we fell in love with it so much, we ended up buying season passes (we don't live in California, but it's a short airplane ride).

I have since also been able to take her on a couple of Disney cruises, and I had never been on a cruise before in my life until I started my practice. We created such good memories.

Our biggest adventure to date was a two-week trip to Europe, just the two of us. We explored Scotland, England, and Ireland. It was such a special experience for me to be able to take her on a trip like that, not stressing about how to afford it or about taking time off. And at the time of writing this book, I just booked an Italian Disney Cruise that I'm taking my daughter and family on. It's all been such a dream come true.

Sometimes it brings me to tears thinking about the life I am able to give my daughter, all because I was willing to admit I wanted to make a lot of money and make a big impact on this world—and put myself out there enough to do so.

Being a single mom is not easy, and having to rely on my own income is not what I expected I'd have to do in life. I'm glad I was able to find a way to make a lot of money so I didn't have to work two jobs trying to make ends meet and hardly have time with my daughter, or be stressed when I am with her because I'm thinking about all the bills I need to pay or wishing I could afford more for her.

Instead, money isn't a concern or a bother anymore. Not only do I get to live abundantly, but I get to teach my daughter that it can be normal to live an abundant life and to set her up for success as she grows up.

Other reasons I am so grateful for the money I make:

- It allows me to live in a beautiful home and safe neighborhood (which is huge for me as a single mom).

- I was able to buy a pink, sparkly Tesla Model X, which brings me and my daughter so much joy every time we drive in it.
- I am able to offer my parents and family support when they need it. I have big goals to be able to pay off my parents' home, cars, and so much for them since they have done so much for me.
- I was able to pay for my entire family (parents and siblings) to go to Hawaii. I was able to give them all something they could not do on their own, and I felt lucky and grateful to do it.
- I am able to pay my team good money and provide opportunities for so many people to make money as my business grows and we keep expanding my team.
- I am able to tip people much better and help those in need.
- I am able to get weekly two-hour massages and take better care of my body.
- I get to buy nice things for myself without needing to stress constantly about the price tag.
- And most importantly, the increasing amount of money I make represents the thousands of therapists I get to help make more money themselves. Each time I make money, I know it represents others I get to help and serve.

This is why I get excited when I make great money. I know that it represents being able to help others in some way.

Expand Your Dreams

I hope this book has allowed you to give yourself permission to expand your visions and dreams.

You are allowed to want more in your life.

You are allowed to charge what you're worth, to say no to sliding scale spots that don't align with your goals, to take time off without guilt, to create a practice that supports your life instead of sacrificing your life to support your practice.

You are allowed to create your dream business and life. You are worthy of all the success you desire. You get to live a thriving, happy, and abundant life. And as you do so, you will then so much more easily be able to impact the lives of your family and everyone around you for the better.

Let this be the moment where you give yourself permission to step into your power, claim your worth, and create the abundant, meaningful life you deserve.

You are worthy. You are capable. You are ready.

I am your biggest cheerleader.

You got this.

Takeaways

- Time to expand your vision on what's possible in life and realize that money is simply a tool that will allow you to reach your goals.

- The more money you make, the more choices you have to be able to help people. When you have more money, you think about it less and instead can think about what really matters to you.

- Money is a tool to be able to make a bigger impact in this world.

- You are worthy of living the most abundant and beautiful life. Let go of the scarcity mindset that therapists often fall into, and tap into the abundance that you deserve.

ACKNOWLEDGMENTS

THANK YOU TO THE TEAM at Illumify Media for providing so much support and help in bringing this book to life—and making my vision as an author not only possible but even easier than I thought it could be. I've been wanting to be an author ever since I was a little girl, and I'm so grateful to finally be able to have the opportunity.

Thank you to Carly Hill for connecting me to Illumify Media, and for being the best mentor possible and teaching me how to have a successful coaching business so I can help even more therapists. Thank you for turning me into a seven-figure business coach, as you have done for yourself. I am forever grateful to you and how my life has changed.

Thank you to each and every participant who has gone through my signature twelve-week program, the Therapist Private Pay Accelerator. I'm truly so grateful and honored you chose to trust me to help you grow your therapy practice. Your success gives me so much joy. You are the reason I do what I do.

Thank you to my entire team at Empowering Therapists. Because of you, so many more therapists are being helped in creating a thriving practice. I truly have the dream team.

Thank you to my parents who provided me a loving and happy home environment growing up, who helped (and saved) me during some of the lowest points in my life, and who continue to love and support me to this day.

And most importantly, thank you to my sweet little daughter for being my best friend and travel buddy and for being the reason I do what I do. Even as I am writing this, you are coming up to me with kisses and love. I love you, baby girl.

ABOUT THE AUTHOR

JESSICA HARRIS IS A THERAPIST and business strategist for therapists. She grew a successful private pay group practice, hiring six other clinicians and attracting between five to ten new full-fee cash-pay clients every week. She eventually sold her practice and today focuses solely on her coaching business, helping other therapists fill their caseload with private pay clients.

Through her twelve-week coaching program, Jessica helps therapists start and/or grow a successful private pay practice. In the process, she helps her clients simplify their marketing and build a strong marketing foundation so they can fill their caseload with private pay clients on an ongoing basis.

Jessica currently resides in South Jordan, Utah, with her beautiful six-year-old daughter. She enjoys lifting weights, going to Disneyland, traveling the world, reading, doing half marathons, being outside, and spending time with loved ones. She has a mission to change the therapist industry and empower therapists by teaching them it's okay to make a shit ton of money and live a better life.

ABOUT EMPOWERING THERAPISTS LLC

Empowering Therapists LLC was created to help therapists who are ready to start and/or grow their private practice and make a better life for themselves. At the time of writing this book, we have helped hundreds of therapists fill their practice with private pay clients, and we are on a mission to help tens of thousands of therapists to do this as well.

Our signature program is the Therapist Private Pay Accelerator, a twelve-week program designed to teach therapists everything they need to know to simplify their marketing, fill their practice with cash pay clients, and enjoy long-term success as a therapist and in their business.

The program includes a recorded course, group coaching calls, weekly 1:1 coaching calls, detailed reviews of your specific marketing strategies, an incredible community of like minded therapists, a private VIP Slack group, and all of the top strategies and tips to fill a private pay practice.

To learn more about how we can help you, please message me on Instagram at @empoweringtherapists or email support@empoweringtherapists.com and my team or I will get back to you.

CONNECT WITH ME

Instagram:

https://www.instagram.com/empoweringtherapists/

Website:

https://www.empoweringtherapists.com/